# THE
# SNIPER'S
# STORY

# THE SNIPER'S STORY

### THE BLACK WATCH FIREARMS SPECIALIST WHO HID A MURDEROUS SECRET

## WENSLEY CLARKSON

FRIDAY

Soho Friday Media Ltd.,
3-4 Temple Bar Business Park,
Strettington Lane, Goodwood,
Chichester, West Sussex,
PO18 OTU

www.sohofriday.com

www.facebook.com/soho.Friday
twitter.com/@sohofriday
www.instagram.com/sohofriday/

First published in paperback in 2019

1 3 5 7 9 10 8 6 4 2

British Library Cataloguing-in-Publication Data:

A catalogue record for this book is available from the British Library.

ISBN: 978-1-913094-03-4

Printed in the UK under supervision of Jellyfish Solutions Ltd

Papers used by Soho Friday Media Ltd. are natural, recyclable products made
from wood grown in sustainable forests. The manufacturing processes conform to
the environmental regulations of the country of origin.

Picture credits: page 1, above and below, Wensley Clarkson (inset top, police file;
inset bottom left and right, J4MR); page 2, *The Orcadian*; page 3, above,
Wensley Clarkson, below left, Kirkwall police, below right, J4MR; page 4 top left
J4MR, remainder on this page Kirkwall police.

Every reasonable effort has been made to trace copyright-holders of
material reproduced in this book, but if any have been inadvertently overlooked
the publishers would be glad to hear from them.

To the good – and bad – residents of the Orkneys
I encountered while writing this book.

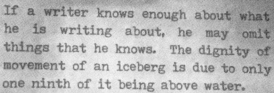

If a writer knows enough about what he is writing about, he may omit things that he knows. The dignity of movement of an iceberg is due to only one ninth of it being above water.

Ernest Hemingway

# THE ORKNEYS AND SCOTLAND

Ferry to
Shetland
Islands

WESTRAY

SANDAY

ATLANTIC OCEAN

ROUSAY          EDAY

● Birsay         STRONSAY

MAINLAND

SHAPINSAY

Kirkwall ●
Stromness       St. Ola  Deerness ●

Scapa Flow      St Mary's ●

Ferry to
Aberdeen

HOY             NORTH SEA

SOUTH
RONALDSAY

Shetland
Islands

0          10 Km

0        5 Miles

● Inverness

SCOTLAND

Ferry to
Thursa

PENTLAND
FIRTH

SCOTLAND   ● John o'Groats

Mull of
Kintyre

NORTHERN
IRELAND

IRELAND

ENGLAND

Archipelago: a group of small islands or an area of sea in
which there are many small islands

# Contents

# Author's Note

THE BLEAK, WINDSWEPT moors surrounding Orkneys' capital Kirkwall sweep across much of the landscape of a sparsely populated cluster of islands that, alongside Shetland, represents the northernmost territory within the boundaries of Great Britain. The temperatures here vary enormously but there is one constant when it comes to the weather – the wind. It was close to fifty miles an hour when I turned up in Kirkwall a couple of days into 2019. The gales were so strong they'd rocked and rolled the ferry across the sea from the mainland and now those same gusts were threatening to slam the front door of my vehicle shut as I struggled to open it.

I'd driven to the Orkneys in my campervan after an informant in Kirkwall advised me to keep a low profile while I was in town and to avoid the local hotels. I soon realised why. Within just twenty-four hours of my arrival, I was passing the same stern faces in the street over and over again and it was clear many already knew what I was doing in the islands' capital. While driving down an isolated country lane on the outskirts of Kirkwall a tractor carrying huge bales of hay coming in the opposite direction almost forced me off the road when I tried to get past it. It seemed deliberate but then again maybe I imagined it. But I certainly didn't imagine the way motorists never thanked me for giving way, unlike in the rest of the UK. One local later explained: 'We only thank the locals here. We're not keen on strangers, so why encourage them?'

Looking extremely carefully both ways when crossing the road in Kirkwall also became a necessary habit because motorists don't slow down for pedestrians in these parts either. And when it came to small talk with the locals, forget it. One old lady I tried to engage while walking my dog in a Kirkwall park looked at me in horror and virtually ran off in the opposite direction.

I should have known. One former policeman on the Orkneys had told me on the phone weeks earlier, 'No one will want to talk to you.' He turned out to be wrong, but only because I refused to take 'No' for an answer and convinced many of my interviewees that I would not reveal their names in this book.

Meanwhile that ferocious wind continued whistling around me wherever I went. Up in the tiny hamlet of St Ola – where many of the characters most relevant to this story lived – the breeze seemed twice as strong as it surged across the bleak landscape and then down onto the vast, historic natural harbour of Scapa Flow. The wind screamed so loudly that it made it doubly hard to hear anyone when I talked to them outside. But then again, some of them clearly didn't want to hear what I was saying in the first place. And not even that gale force wind could drown out the abuse I got from those who refused point-blank to help and slammed their doors in my face. Many who knew this story later said they were amazed some of the characters involved hadn't waved a gun in my face because – as I was about to discover – firearms are prevalent in these parts.

As I reached the end of my trip to the Orkneys, I found myself struck by the gritty, independent character of these people. It became clear why so many had turned their backs on the cold, harsh reality of what happened here in the summer of 1994. It was simply easier for them to bury their heads in the sand once they were convinced that the killer in their midst was of no threat to anyone else.

This story takes place over a period of twenty-five years. Many of the pivotal characters started as children and are now middle-aged. Others have gone from early middle age to pensioners during that time. No wonder some of those I encountered seemed virtually broken by the time I reached out to them.

My undeniable curiosity about the murder of Shamsuddin Mahmood had been first fuelled some years earlier. I was investigating the activities of the Brink's Mat gold bullion robbery gang for a TV documentary and discovered that one of the detectives involved had retired to live in Kirkwall. When I met former Scotland Yard Flying Squad officer Bill Miller in 2015, he told me, 'There's a big crime story here in Kirkwall you should write a book about . . .' I was stunned that a place so tranquil and isolated could be at the centre of such a cold-blooded murder. Then as I began investigating the background to the case, I realised I'd stumbled on one of the most disturbing and chilling crimes ever committed in Britain.

## THE SNIPER'S STORY

Ultimately, this book revolves around a way of life; a tough mentality that has been deeply influenced by the islanders' close relationship with the British armed services. Many believe to this day that serving the nation is more important than even the most heinous of crimes.

Unpeeling this story has left me with myriad impressions of the Orkneys and all the characters you are about to 'meet'. But as I researched and then wrote the book, I realised some of my sources had shady, ulterior motives and my aim has always been to show this murder story in a balanced light, not a version warped by the evil intent of people on both sides of the divide.

So the story you are about to read may not be the one that most Orcadians would have preferred to be told. But it is the nearest to the truth about a case that has left a 'mark' on everyone it has touched, from the hard-pressed local police force to the families of both the victim and his killer.

During the course of researching this book I've been taken into the confidence of many people who, for obvious reasons, would prefer to remain anonymous. I have respected the wishes of those individuals, and I need only say that my decision to do so was as much to protect the guilty as the innocent, as well as ensuring the safety of these individuals in such a close-knit community. As a result, some of the scenes depicted here represent a combination of facts reconstructed to reflect the events of the past twenty-five years. Certain characterisations, incidents, locations and dialogue were composited for dramatic purposes. By writing this book I also hope, in a sense, to wipe away the cobwebs of an event that has overshadowed everything else on these islands for a quarter of a century.

High up on a hillside near Kirkwall, overlooking the historic bay of Scapa Flow, is a small cluster of houses that overlook the wreck of a British battleship that was sunk just a few weeks after the outbreak of World War II with the loss of nearly one thousand lives.

That war grave unequivocally links the troubled past of the Orkney Islands with the real-life crime you're going to read about. We need to begin this story eighty years ago, on a cold, starless night when a ruthless German submarine commander ripped the heart out of this quiet, deserted paradise.

Wensley Clarkson, London, 2019

# Introduction

## SCAPA FLOW, THE ORKNEYS, 12.45 A.M., 14 OCTOBER 1939

GERMAN SUBMARINE *U-47* – under the command of legendary *Kapitän* Günther Prien – glided just below the surface of the narrow sea channel with surprising ease. It was high tide, past midnight and *U-47* had encountered no resistance as it passed more than a dozen fighting ships before turning north to where HMS *Royal Oak*, HMS *Pegasus* and possibly HMS *Iron Duke* were said to be moored.

When the first torpedo struck HMS *Royal Oak* at 12.58 a.m., the dull thud confused the sailors. They presumed the muffled explosions were an onboard problem, perhaps a blast in the paint store. They certainly didn't realise they were being attacked by a German U-boat that had sneaked into the very heart of British sovereign territory. A second salvo from *U-47* failed to find its target but the confusion surrounding that first hit gave Prien extra minutes to return to his firing position, reload and fire a third salvo. This discharge landed a direct hit amidships.

# THE SNIPER'S STORY

Such were the ferocity of the explosions that HMS *Royal Oak's* lights went out and she keeled over almost instantly. There had been fine weather earlier and all of the ship's hatches were open. The *Royal Oak* would have taken longer to sink and more lives would have been saved if those watertight hatches had indeed been closed but it was standard procedure to have them open when docked in a supposedly safe harbour-like Scapa Flow.

As the enormous ship rolled, its gun barrels shifted, pulling the vessel even more rapidly beneath the surface. Water gushed through those open hatches and many men asleep in their bunks had little chance. Less than a minute after being hit, the battleship sank with hundreds of sailors screaming in terror and fighting for their lives. Some of them tried to swim for shore, through thick fuel oil and in freezing temperatures. A total of 834 men were lost that night. Some are buried in a nearby Royal Naval cemetery but many remain in the wreck on the seabed of Scapa Flow.

As a direct result of this audacious attack, German U-boats became known to many during World War II as 'snipers of the sea', which is especially significant because these quiet, sparsely populated islands have had strong links through the military to lone marksmen for more than one hundred years. Some believe that the isolation experienced by many in the Orkneys has given islanders the perfect mentality to become snipers, making life and death decisions in a split second. And many also believe that this community has never truly recovered from that attack by *U-47*, which struck fear and trepidation into so many Orcadians. Many locals believed that packs of 'grey wolves' – as U-boats were also known – could appear at any moment to destroy more ships in Scapa

Flow. And many of those living in houses overlooking the harbour during World War II rarely slept through the night for fear of another such attack.

Adolf Hitler hailed *U-47*'s *Kapitän* Prien a hero for his daring attack on the *Oak*, which was Germany's way of telling Britain they could destroy anything they wanted on British soil. Prien was even nicknamed *Der Stier von* Scapa Flow ('The Bull of Scapa Flow') and the emblem of a snorting bull was painted on the conning tower of *U-47*. So, Hitler's influence on these barren, often windswept islands is undeniable and – as you will read further into this story – the legacy of the Nazis even found a number of unlikely disciples in the Orkneys.

Those who live in Scapa Flow today say that some days the wind whistles so furiously across the surface of the sea that it often sounds like people screaming. 'They say it's those poor men drowning after that U-boat struck,' said one Orcadian. 'Their ghosts remind us we must never forget what happened.'

The war grave wreck of the *Royal Oak* in Scapa Flow is marked by one solitary orange buoy. Twelve metres beneath the surface the upturned, battered hull can just be seen through the musty waters at low tide. On the port side of the lower hull are two vast, jagged torpedo holes, testament to the HMS *Royal Oak* sinking so quickly with such a huge loss of lives. No wonder that the story of *U-47*'s attack on the *Oak* is told to just about every child who lives within a few miles of this eerie, abandoned naval base. And like all of us damaged by our past, that attack by *U-47* left a chilling legacy on many Orcadians, who to this very day fear that 'bad strangers' will do it all over again.

Scapa Flow resident Eddy Rossheard about the submarine's

daring raid many times as a child. He was so bewitched by the story and the area's military history that he settled his young family in a house overlooking Scapa Flow. It's said that many U-boat commanders launched their most ferocious torpedo attacks to the music of Wagner. Some even believe that if rock 'n' roll had existed during the last world war then it would have been top of every *kapitän*'s musical choices.

As it happens, rock band Megadeth contributed much of the soundtrack to the teenage life of Eddy Ross's son, Michael, the pivotal character in the story you are about to read. His musical choices give this true crime drama a unique rhythm all of its own. The ups and downs of Michael Ross's life; his determination to make his father proud at all costs; the discipline instilled in him by that same father. Yet the rebellious streak that ultimately may well have cost Michael Ross his liberty.

It's all here and it all began in this strange, often inhospitable land where the locals firmly believe that nature literally broke their islands off from the rest of the United Kingdom thousands of years ago, so they could be left to their own devices.

But then no one in the Orkneys could have ever dreamt they would be plunged into a real-life murder mystery on a warm summer's evening in June 1994. From the local *Herald* newspaper:

### POLICE HUNT FOR HITMAN AFTER MURDER OF WAITER

*4 June 1994*

*The murder of a waiter in an Indian restaurant in Orkney could have been the work of a contract killer, police said yesterday.*

*The killer, wearing a hood and balaclava, burst into the crowded Mumtaz restaurant in Kirkwall on Thursday night, made straight for the waiter and shot him in the face before running off.*

*Police last night refused to name the dead man. But the restaurant owner, Mr Moina Miah, said he was Shamol Mahmood, aged twenty-four or twenty-five, who moved to Orkney from London seven weeks ago. Yesterday police reinforcements, including senior detectives, were drafted into Orkney from Inverness to join the hunt for the gunman. With a watch being kept on airfields and harbours, every passenger leaving the islands by plane or ferry was questioned.*

*Orkney's senior police officer, Chief Inspector Alistair MacLeod, said there was a possibility that the gunman had already left the islands. 'There would be so many ways of doing that – by fishing boat, yacht, ferry, light aircraft or conventional air service,' he said. 'But there is still the possibility that he's gone to ground and will lie low for a week before trying to leave as if nothing has happened. This was an extraordinary and horrific thing to have happened in a community like Orkney. We simply have no idea what the background to the killing is. We cannot rule out the possibility that this was a contract killing. We have nothing so far to suggest that it is, but we certainly can't rule that out.'*

*He said a number of people had been questioned at Kirkwall police station after officers took them away from a bed-and-breakfast establishment at St Margaret's Hope in South Ronaldsay. But they were later released.*

*Mr Miah said, 'We won't feel safe until they catch this man.'*

*Mr Miah, his family and eighteen-year-old waiter Khukon Uddin have gone into hiding at a house in Kirkwall. 'He didn't have any enemies and we haven't got any enemies,' Mr Miah added. 'As far as I know no one has got a grudge against us. We are now really scared – we think that that whoever did this could come after us as well.'*

*Mr Uddin said he had been watching a video in a room above the restaurant at the time of the killing. 'I came down and saw him lying on the ground and bleeding from terrible head wounds,' he said. 'All I can think of is that this was a racial attack by someone who didn't like the colour of our skin. But we are terrified that this could happen to us. We feel we need protection until this man is caught.'*

*Orkney's first murder for twenty-five years has shocked the community. The island's council convener, Hugh Halcro-Johnston, said, 'Everyone is stunned by this. This is just not something that happens in Orkney. It's something we see on television and something we hear about happening in other areas.'*

The vicious slaying of an innocent man was about to tear apart an entire community.

# Prologue

## Scapa Flow, the Orkneys, June 1994, a few days after the murder

THE WIND WAS so strong that it could have bent trees double if there had been any trees on the bare, desolate moors and hillsides overlooking the vast empty natural harbour of Scapa Flow.

In the distance, a breathless, hooded man wearing a military-style backpack charged manically towards a flock of sheep. He ducked around the animals as they gathered in a small flock by the corner of a large field next to a big water trough. He jumped over a gate and dropped expertly behind an ancient stone wall before checking to see if anyone was behind him. Then he glanced up at a cluster of houses off in the distance, knowing full well they were too far away for anyone to see him.

For a few moments, the hooded figure waited and further scanned the area in front and behind to make sure the coast was still clear. Satisfied it was, the man hunched down even lower, dropped down and started weaving his way across the field. It was as if he feared a sniper had his weapon trained on him. As he ran, the hooded figure stayed alongside the ancient wall, which provided him with cover. He then jumped over the wall before darting across the next field. As he did so, the noise of the crashing of the waves in Scapa Flow got louder. But he didn't stop. Instead he accelerated even faster alongside the wall towards the sea.

Breathing heavily, he finally stopped at the cliff top and looked down at the choppy waters, a place that had seen so much death and destruction in the past. But on this windy summer's day in 1994, Scapa Flow was empty except for one lone fishing vessel bobbing about on the waves as it struggled slowly towards the quayside near a golden sand beach close to the rolling hills where so many young Orcadians got their first taste of a regimented lifestyle.

Having stopped by that cliff edge, the hooded figure removed his backpack, sat down, and his eyes snapped around the bay just as he had done so many times during his childhood. After all, his family home overlooked this idyllic setting. Then the man took a balaclava out of his backpack and held it in his hand momentarily as he looked out towards the sea. The troubled history of Scapa Flow had always fascinated him and his family. It had even had a direct influence on his own most important life decisions.

Still sitting on the edge of the cliff, the hooded man reached across the mossy grassland and picked up a small rock. Then he stood up and moved closer to the edge of the cliff. No doubt a million thoughts were rushing through his mind. The man grimaced, then forced the small rock deep into the balaclava and scrunched it up in a ball in his fist. Below him waves were crashing noisily onto the rocks. He pulled back his arm and then threw the balaclava as high and far out as he could manage.

For a nanosecond, the balaclava froze in mid-air as it was caught by a strong crosswind. Then it fell rapidly down towards the water. The hooded figure couldn't take his eyes off it until it hit the sea with a small splash and sank beneath the choppy surface of the cold, bleak North Atlantic.

**Euphrates River, Fallujah, Iraq, November 2004**

This water's warmer but it's tainted with yellow mustiness. The sound of gunfire crackles in the distance. We're on the banks of Fallujah's most notorious waterway. Nearby is a closely packed group of crumbling houses, which allied troops know are providing good camouflage for insurgent fighters.

Heavily armed British squaddies from the Black Watch regiment mingle among Iraqi civilians on a side street as armoured cars with gunners in turrets stand guard.

To the south of the city, US troops can be heard firing 81mm mortars that thud into the ground as their units surge towards the western approaches and the nearby Jurf Kas Sukrbridge. Back on a rooftop among those buildings on the edge of the Euphrates River, a British army sniper watches for his opportunity to fire as a soldier spotter next to him holds a camera to capture footage for the record while also scanning the area for the enemy. All around them the sounds of the streets blend in with male Arabic voices as the sniper and his spotter talk.

'Anything?' asks the sniper in a broad Scottish accent.

'Looks all clear to me but you never know.'

Just then, the Black Watch sniper and his spotter notice something glinting in the searing midday sun more than three hundred metres ahead of them on an opposing rooftop.

'That's him,' says the sniper, his finger stroking the trigger of his rifle.

'*Allahu Akbar!*'(God is great) exclaim the mocking Brits. Moments later, the glint disappears from view. Another insurgent sniper has been extinguished in the dust of war-torn Iraq.

As one Iraq war vet later explained, 'The worst enemy of a sniper is another sniper. Our snipers are hunting these guys – I guarantee you this is happening as we speak.'

As they say, the best defence is good offence. And this British army sniper had learned how to kill from a very early age.

# Part One

# Father and Son

6 To create a hero is to create a self. 9
— Robert Penn Warren

6 Childhood is measured out by sounds and smells and sights, before the dark hour of reason grows. 9
–John Betjeman

# 1.

## Falls Road, Belfast, Northern Ireland, late summer 1969

THE TELESCOPIC LENS panned around looking for the perfect target as a finger stroked the trigger gently. The weapon eventually locked onto a young British squaddie and began closely following him as he patrolled the back streets of one of the most dangerous places in the world.

Back in his lair – a first floor window – the shooter grimaced and then squeezed the trigger. A brief hissing of air escaping from the rifle was the only sound it made. Two hundred yards away, the young soldier didn't even hear the faint whistling noise as the bullet spun through the air at 1,700 miles per hour. A split second later it ripped the surface of his flak jacket and grazed his left arm, but he didn't flinch. Instead, he ducked down in exactly the way he'd been trained to. Then he briefly turned and squinted towards the shooter, before weaving in the direction the bullet had been fired.

Turning over dustbins and pushing mothers and their children out of the way, the young soldier kept his focus on the shooter's exact location. Watching all this from his post a few yards away on the same deadly road was Black Watch soldier Edmond Andrew Ross – Eddy to all his family and friends. He later said he'd witnessed something that day he would never forget for the rest of his life.

'He'd only been shot in the arm,' Eddy Ross later told this author, 'so this little terrier Brit went after his attackers. He hunted them down and killed two or three of them. That's what I call bravery.'

Eddy Ross liked telling accounts of his battles in Belfast to anyone prepared to listen. He learned on the streets of Northern Ireland that being armed around the clock and being prepared to shoot to kill was the only effective way to protect yourself. As a result, Eddy was – and still is – a self-proclaimed gun fanatic. Since the age of twelve he'd harboured a keen interest in all types of firearms. So to find himself with the elite Black Watch regiment guarding the deadly streets of Northern Ireland during the height of the Troubles was, in a sense, a dream come true.

The Black Watch served in the Province as part of Operation Banner. The regiment was frequently a major target for the Provisional Irish Republican Army (PIRA) and the Irish National Liberation Army (INLA). Eddy's regiment had been devastated when one of their lance corporals was shot dead by another sniper in east Belfast and then there was a young private killed by a remote-control device while on foot patrol in Dungannon, County Tyrone. Any shooting or killing by an enemy sniper was particularly hard for the Black Watch regiment to deal with because they themselves had been considered masters of the 'art' of long-distance killing for almost a century. But the tables were being turned on them. As one British army sniper later explained, 'A sniper – whatever side they are on – is a killing machine. He should feel no emotion about his victim. It's cold-blooded and that killing in Belfast rocked the Black Watch boys because no one, literally, had seen it coming.'

Eddy Ross was no doubt as profoundly moved as all his fellow soldiers were by the fatalities suffered by his regiment in Northern Ireland and those memories stayed with him for his entire life. He realised that a sniper's job was not only to kill the enemy but to destroy their confidence and fill them with fear. It was psychological warfare on the most basic level. Ross was a lean and wiry character who'd been well-trained to keep a low centre of gravity while moving through Northern Ireland's deadly streets where danger seemed to lurk on every corner. Colleagues later remembered Eddy as being constantly alert to everything around him. As one former colleague later explained, 'Eddy never switched off. He watched everyone's back all the time. Being in Northern Ireland no doubt taught him not to trust anyone. But you can't blame him for that. The Irish Republican Army (IRA) wanted to kill as many British soldiers as they could. It really was a matter of kill or be killed.'

Eddy and his fellow soldiers had even been trained specifically how to deal with interrogation by the 'enemy' if they were ever captured. Eddy believed he would never crack in the face of any violent threats, however harsh. No doubt he promised himself he'd pass on those skills to any children he might have in the future. Ross was immensely proud of his six tours of duty in Northern Ireland in the late '60s and early '70s. He adored the distinct sound of the Black Watch pipes and drums that were played every morning before he and his unit hit the troubled streets on foot patrol. He also knew the Black Watch regimental 'collect' by heart.

> *O God, whose strength setteth fast the mountains,*
> *Lord of the hills to whom we lift our eyes,*
> *Grant us grace that we, of The Black Watch, once*
> *chosen to watch the mountains of an earthly kingdom,*
> *may stand fast in the faith and be strong,*
> *Until we come to the heavenly Kingdom of Him*
> *Who has bidden us watch and pray*
> *Thy son, our saviour and Lord.*
> *Amen*

There was another side to soldier Eddy Ross. He was also renowned for his ability to use gallows humour to cope with some very dangerous moments. Naturally, it endeared him greatly to his fellow soldiers.

As the bloodshed spread and Catholics across the province found themselves under attack by groups of Protestants, young soldiers like Eddy Ross found themselves at the centre of what he always described as a full-scale war. Northern Ireland had fast evolved into a vicious cycle of terrorism and repression as Catholics set up no-go areas in their districts of cities such as Londonderry and Belfast, as well as other towns across the province. As Eddy later explained, 'It was deadly out there. Politicians like to call it a conflict but to us it was war. There was no other word for it. We took our lives into our hands every day.'

Ross primarily covered Belfast and the so-called 'bandit country' of South Armagh. The Black Watch chalked up more tours in Northern Ireland than virtually any other British army regiment. But as one Black Watch veteran later said, 'We were tough bastards and as Scotsmen we understood the battles more than most but that didn't make it any easier to handle.'

Eddy Ross never complained about such things as danger. He is so proud of his and his family's association with the Black Watch that he still uses china tea mugs emblazoned with the regiment's motto and badge to this day. 'It's in yer blood. I'm Black Watch through and through,' he said many years later.

The Royal Scots and the Black Watch regiments were at the heart of events that led to an impromptu curfew on the Lower Falls Road in 1970, an event said to have hardened the Republican stance towards the army. Tipped off that there was a cache of weapons at a house on Balkan Street, soldiers from a Royal Scots support company moved in to conduct a search and , after finding nineteen guns, they came under attack and retaliated with their batons. As rioting spread, grenades and petrol bombs were thrown, CS gas was used and a fierce gun battle ensued. Reinforcements from the Black Watch including Eddy Ross, newly arrived in Belfast, and other regiments were drafted– and at 10p,m. the decision was made to impose a curfew, with the instruction given to clear and dominate the area.

The curfew lasted for three days and was broken when women marched into the Falls Road waving shopping bags, loaves of bread and milk. By then three Catholic civilians and a visitor from England had died, seventy-five people, including fifteen soldiers had been injured, 337 people had been arrested and a huge cache of firearms, grenades and ammunition was recovered. In the aftermath, there were allegations that soldiers from the Scottish regiments had used excessive force, deliberately destroying religious objects in the homes they searched. There was no doubt British soldiers were guilty of some questionable acts during the Troubles but as Eddy Ross would say, 'It was a war out there.'

Still in his early twenties, Eddy Ross had deep-set lines on his face that made him appear older. It gave him an air of maturity compared to many of his contemporaries. This had earlier marked him out as a potential leader and led to him becoming one of the youngest-ever sergeants in the Black Watch. One of Ross's associates later explained, 'Eddy was in many ways a natural leader but only to those on his own level. Some officers found him cocky, arrogant and verging on being disrespectful. Eddy said they were just insecure because they knew he was brighter than them.'

With the young soldiers of the British army struggling to keep the peace while risking their own lives, it still outrages old soldiers like Eddy Ross to this day that no one seemed very grateful back then. As an article in regimental magazine *The Red Hackle* explained back in 1976, 'He (the soldier) is ordered onto the streets of Belfast with a weapon in his hands, live rounds in his pouches, enormous powers at his disposal, and then told that he is dealing with normal British subjects. He has been trained as a soldier, how to observe, how to seek out a target and how to shoot. Suddenly he is thrown into a situation where he has to make the terrible decision between being polite and firm at one moment and shooting to kill in self-defence at another.' A wry comment of the time was that a mistake made by a young soldier on the streets of Belfast could plunge Northern Ireland into chaos or bring down the government in London. It really was as serious as that.

No doubt, Eddy Ross's experiences in Northern Ireland would have deadened his senses in a way, as most soldiers who have served in conflict zones would attest. One explained, 'When bullets are flying all around you and you know the locals would love nothing more than to kill you it certainly hardens you up. You learn not to look on those people as human beings in the normally accepted term. They are the enemy. Shoot first or be shot. It was as simple as that. So it's hard to adjust back to normal life once you leave the services. People just don't seem to realise that.'

There were numerous experiences of life in the Black Watch that would stay with Eddy Ross for a lifetime. He'd eventually pass them down to his own sons in much the same way some parents read children's books each night to their offspring. The grisly, bullet-ridden fairy tales of Belfast were what drove Eddy on as a parent. He hoped his own children would follow his path in life and this was just one of his ways of ensuring that happened.

After his promotion to sergeant, Eddy Ross did six months training as an armourer at Borden, in Hampshire, at the army's school of electrical and mechanical engineering. No doubt his childhood experiences with guns back in the Orkneys greatly helped his career in the army. He had enjoyed a happy childhood near the Orkney capital Kirkwall. Now here he was, in his early twenties, with a licence to kill. Others who served with Eddy Ross later said he had a genuine thirst for knowledge about guns. He'd learned from a very young age not to fear them but to use them because they could save his life.

Sergeant Eddy Ross was eventually seconded to the 1st Battalion Royal Green Jackets based at Celle in what was then

West Germany, between 1972 and 1974. His knowledge of armour had turned him into a sought-after specialist on the base. In July 1974, Ross left the army and returned to the Orkneys. It seemed that he was looking for something more peaceful, with a view to marrying and having a family and settling down back in the place of his birth. Today, he makes it crystal clear he considers his days as a soldier as having been 'magical'. He thrived on the responsibility of being a soldier and his respected knowledge as an expert armourer gave him additional status within the Black Watch regiment. He also completely agreed with the armed forces chiefs and even the politicians who insisted that sending the troops in was (and still is) a vitally important aspect of policing the world.

Ross's fondness for firearms was undoubtedly originally fuelled by the gun culture that had existed in the Orkneys for hundreds of years. And he had no intention of putting his love of guns away because he'd left the army. He planned to shoot for pleasure on gun ranges and go rabbit-hunting on the desolate hills overlooking the slightly grim red-and-grey-bricked buildings of Kirkwall. Just one month after leaving the Black Watch regiment, in August, Ross joined the Northern Constabulary on the Orkneys. It couldn't have been more different from the grim and deadly often urban street warfare of Northern Ireland. Ross had been brought up close to the natural deep-water harbour of Scapa Flow and all its ghosts. Many, including Ross himself, believed Scapa Flow perfectly reflected the evolvement of the islands going all the way back to Viking times.

During Eddy's childhood, two Martello towers – a type of fort – on either side of the entrance to the waters of Scapa Flow were the only remaining evidence of the area's need for defence during World War II. Eddy and many of his contemporaries were brought up to believe it was their right to bear arms at all times. Many Orcadians not only accepted guns in their society but actively encouraged them.

As a PC, Eddy Ross soon earned himself a reputation as a quietly spoken but very firm local bobby on the beat, dealing with everything from poaching to cattle rustling. But many say he was a stickler for the rules and always made sure that everyone knew that he had the power to throw them in a jail cell if they defied him. This shoot-first-ask-questions-later mentality no doubt evolved from Eddy Ross's experiences in Northern Ireland. 'He wasn't one to stop and listen much. You were either right or wrong in his world and that was that,' said one of his former colleagues.

Within a relatively short time of settling back in the Kirkwall area of the Orkneys, Eddy Ross married his sweetheart Moira and together they bought a house overlooking Eddy's beloved Scapa Flow. Eddy called the property *Tjörn*, an ancient Norse word meaning 'pool of water'. It's often said that the name of a house can help protect it from the elements and no doubt Eddy Ross believed that the ancient spirits of the forefathers of the Orkneys would ensure that all those living in *Tjörn* would be safe, including the baby that Moira announced she was expecting. It was the spring of 1978.

# 2.

ON THE ATLANTIC-FACING, west side of the Orkneys, the coastlines are renowned for their dramatic sea-cliffs and awe-inspiring panoramic views, whereas the eastern coast is more gentle and features long, sandy beaches that wouldn't look out of place in the Caribbean. But overlooking all these coastlines are the smooth contours of the bleak land honed by the action of the retreating Scandinavian ice sheets, which finally disappeared some ten thousand years ago. They've turned the lowlands of the Orkneys into open, treeless moors ideal for tracking prey.

The Orkneys themselves consist of more than seventy islands and islets but only about twenty of them are actually inhabited. Humans have lived on them for about 8,800 years, according to archeological evidence from Mesolithic times. Scandinavian clans dominated the area from the eighth century, using the islands as a base for incursions onto enemy coastlines. In the late fourteenth century, the archipelago became associated with the kingdom of Scotland.

Groups of fanatics have always thrived in these windswept, deserted islands. A classic example were the Freemasons. They chose to set up the second-ever Masonic lodge in the world, near Kirkwall, back in 1736. Called Lodge Kirkwall Kilwinning No. 382, it predated the charter from the grand lodge of Scotland of 1740. Even today, Freemasons' meetings are held throughout the year at the austere headquarters on the edge of Kirkwall. It's well-known that many of Eddy Ross's police colleagues were members of the Freemasons as was (and still is) the case throughout much of the UK. Local membership also included judges and lawyers. Though the Freemasons have always been looked upon by outsiders as a mysterious and secretive organisation, most members insist to this day it is a society of men concerned with moral and spiritual values. Members are said to be taught its principles through a series of ritual dramas in the form of two-part plays, which are learnt by heart and performed by members within each lodge. These plays follow ancient forms, using stonemasons' customs and tools as allegorical guides.

New members relish mastering the art of the Freemasons' handshake, which involves putting the thumb between the first and second finger and pressing the knuckle on the middle finger. This indicates that the person in question is 'on the third degree' – Mason-speak for being a member. When criminals met a policeman they thought was a Mason, they'd make a point of using that handshake very carefully to ascertain his or her membership.

Some Freemason police officers have in the past inferred that their membership meant they were above the law. As one police officer recently explained, 'Many criminals cynically manipulated themselves into Freemasonry as if it was the right pub for them to be seen at. Some police officer members were outraged by the presence of known criminals in their ranks, others saw it as an ideal opportunity to pick up new informants.'

The Freemasons themselves had a lot of power on the Orkneys back in the 1970s. At the Kirkwall branch was one of the oldest and most important Masonic artifacts in the world, hanging in the temple in their headquarters. Known as the Kirkwall Scroll, it was made of three pieces of strong linen (some suggest sailcloth) sewn together and hand-painted throughout. The complete hanging cloth was eighteen feet and six inches long, and five feet and six inches wide. On its central strip were around one hundred Masonic symbols. The two outer strips appeared to have ancient maps.

The Freemasons might have been immensely proud of their ancient connections to the Orkneys but none of this impressed Eddy Ross. He was more attracted to membership of the local British legion where his first love, the army, was represented by numerous local old soldiers who'd fought in various conflicts all the way back to World War I. This was the place where Eddy could enjoy a pint with like-minded people and exchange war stories, literally. No doubt his experiences in Northern Ireland earned him the utmost respect from his contemporaries at the British Legion.

The Legion was founded in 1921 as a voice for the ex-service community. It represented a merger between three organisations: the Comrades of the Great War, the National Association of Discharged Sailors and Soldiers and the National Federation of Discharged and Demobilised Sailors and Soldiers, and incorporated the fundraising department of the Officers' Association. Initially, the British Legion was run and frequented by Britain's upper class, but gradually over the years that changed as club premises were opened all over the UK. After World War II, membership grew rapidly, reaching three million by 1950. It had declined to half a million elderly survivors by the late 1970s, but PC Eddy Ross had developed a 'legend' all of his own that gave him real status in Kirkwall, especially among all the old servicemen vets who were members of the Legion.

Meanwhile, he continually refused the Freemasons' invitation. In later life, Eddy would openly voice his suspicion and mistrust of the masons and it is certainly true that by not joining them, he may have distanced himself from a lot of his police colleagues.

'But that was typical Eddy Ross,' said one former colleague. 'He didn't want to join a "club" where he'd be right at the bottom of the so-called food chain. He wanted to be a leader of men, not a sheep or a nobody. That's the way Eddy has always been.'

On Monday, 28 August 1978, Eddy and his wife Moira celebrated the birth of their first child, a son called Michael Joseph. It was by all accounts a relatively simple and uncomplicated event. At the time, the US president was Jimmy Carter but America must have seemed a world away from the Orkneys. Talk of the continuation of Nixon's 'war on drugs' in the United States would no doubt have seemed as relevant as outer space. Drugs and serious crime were something that happened in big cities a long way from the Orkneys. Ross had by this time put the troubled streets of Northern Ireland behind him and created his very own version of domestic bliss. That modest house that Eddy and Moira had chosen before Michael's birth was the perfect place to bring up children, as far as he was concerned.

It was located in a quiet hilltop hamlet called St Ola, just a couple of miles outside Kirkwall but a world away from the busy town. From Eddy's perspective, the house represented his own special version of paradise overlooking his beloved Scapa Flow. It was big enough for the children he fully expected to follow Michael. The property wasn't plush by anyone's standards but its sitting room directly overlooked Scapa Flow, that mysterious stretch of water so steeped in Orkney's history. It would be a constant reminder to Eddy Ross of the glory and disasters of Britain's wartime past. He must have considered himself extremely lucky in the late 1970s. He had a beautiful young family, a responsible job and a nice home. What more could you ask for?

Looking out over Scapa Flow and its colourful military history, even sparked in Eddy Ross some admiration for the courage of the *U-47 Kapitän* and its crew, who'd slipped into Scapa Flow and humiliated the British navy just a few weeks after the outbreak of World War II. He admired the skills of the German engineers who'd built those sophisticated snipers of the sea. And the pull of the army, in particular the Black Watch regiment, was so strong for Eddy Ross that he'd already mapped out his baby son Michael's future career.

One former police colleague explained, 'Eddy knew what he wanted his son Michael to do virtually from the moment he was born. He wanted him to join the Black Watch when he left school. Eddy believed it would give the boy a proper future beyond the Orkneys.' And there certainly seemed to be some wisdom in Eddy Ross's plans for his baby son. The same former police colleague said, 'There were no proper jobs here. Michael would have ended up working in a local supermarket car park and maybe then being promoted to shelf-stacking.

No, Eddy knew the army would give Michael an opportunity to be something special.'

On the Orkneys, Eddy Ross soon found that being a policeman earned him a definite measure of respect. Although some colleagues later recall Eddy Ross as being 'slightly detached' when it came to the social side of his new career, especially if it involved anything to do with the Freemasons.

But the British Legion was a different matter altogether. One Kirkwall club member recalled, 'Eddy definitely preferred the company of old soldiers to most coppers. I think he trusted us more. The police force contained many highly ambitious characters and Eddy found all the politics irritating. He wasn't very good at arse-licking when it came to his bosses. He just wanted to go out every day, do his job, help keep the streets peaceful and safe and then come here for a pint and enjoy a gentle family life up in St Ola.'

Eddy's fondness for firearms led to him joining the Orkney Smallbore Association's hooting range where he spent many Saturdays sharpening up his skills as a marksman. One police colleague later recalled how he once asked Eddy why he bothered with firearms when the police were not even allowed to carry them. 'Eddy just shrugged his shoulders and ignored my question,' the colleague said. 'In many ways Eddy was a gun-nut in the nicest possible way. He didn't try and push his views on other people and we certainly didn't feel in any way threatened by his large collection of guns, as long he didn't bring any of them to work.'

The 1970s were about to give way to the 1980s and Eddy was living in a 1950s' time-warp. He dressed in tweed jackets and highly polished brogues when off duty. He was old-fashioned in many of his beliefs and habits. 'Eddy didn't much trust the modern world but that's quite easy to do when you live in a place like the Orkneys,' one Orcadian said. 'Back then it was even more isolated than it is now. We only had a couple of TV stations and local radio at the time. You could do and feel and think what you liked. In Eddy's case and, as with many of his contemporaries who'd been in the armed services, the modern world was something to be viewed with great suspicion.'

Out on the main shopping streets of the centre of Kirkwall back in the late 1970s, the latest fashions didn't appear in the store windows much. One longtime Kirkwall resident explained, 'People dressed more or less the same way they had since the end of the World War II. Mini-skirts were frowned upon, especially by parents of teenage children. Colours were dark not bright. Most folk round here didn't like anything out of the ordinary. We didn't care for new fads and the so-called swinging sixties never really got up here.'

Eddy Ross and many others like him undoubtedly preferred it that way. As a beat policeman in a closely knit, sparsely populated community, strangers were viewed with suspicion because they brought trouble with them from the mainland. Recreational-drug use, for example, was something that happened 'down south'. However, Eddy and his colleagues at Kirkwall police were warned to keep a close eye out for anyone who might be either on drugs or selling them. 'That meant viewing visitors with even more suspicion because they were the only suspects when it came to drugs,' one Kirkwall resident later explained. Ross and many young parents like him on the Orkneys were grateful to be living in such a quiet, reserved environment where their children would not be exposed to such vices. The same Kirkwall resident said,

## THE SNIPER'S STORY

'The police here treated certain types of strangers with great suspicion, as if they were dangerous interlopers out to destroy our beautiful islands.'

Some of Eddy's former police colleagues believed that Eddy's rigidness as a policeman was a reflection of his own mistrust of strangers. One co-worker said, 'Eddy would often stop visitors and tell them off for petty infractions like walking on the wrong side of a country lane. Some were quite scared of him because he represented authority in a very narrow kind of way.'

Meanwhile, Ross's social life continued to revolve around the British Legion clubhouse on Junction Road, in the centre of Kirkwall. One member recalled, 'The bar in that place was always teeming with old soldiers. It was a social hub for the towns ex-servicemen and Eddy thrived in such an atmosphere. People looked up to him. He liked that.'

One evening in 1984 Eddy got talking to a recently retired former marine called Jim Spence at the Legion clubhouse bar. Spence had been based at Condor, in Arbroath, working mainly on anti-tank duties. He'd also been put into the armoury as the base store man, which meant he dealt with actual weapons. The two men got on well and were soon swapping war stories. Eddy made no secret of his continual interest in weapons and ammunition. Many of his British Legion contemporaries also belonged to the Orkney Smallbore Association. Spence offered Ross 9mm ammunition he'd taken with him from his locker when he left the marines with a box of standard .22 bullets. Spence wanted to get rid of them because he didn't have an armoury certificate and was not a member of the club at which Eddy did his target practice. Spence had moved back in with his elderly mother in Kirkwall after leaving the marines in 1981. After she died, the bullets in question were 'just thrown into a cupboard in my bedroom,' Spence recalled. 'I knew that Eddy was very keen on guns and I told him about the boxes of ammunition I had and asked him if he would get rid of them for me.'

A couple of days later, Spence gave Ross all three boxes of ammunition in a car park in Albert Street, in the centre of Kirkwall. Ross said, 'Jim had no interest in shooting at this time and knew I did and that I used 9mm. I don't know if Jim had any other ammunition but I don't think he would have.'

Spence thought he was doing Ross a favour by giving him all that ammunition. He had no idea how that decision would one day come back to haunt him.

# 3.

THE STUNNING LOCATION of Eddy Ross's home over-looking Scapa Flow may well have influenced his interest in the Nazis. At the Legion clubhouse, many old vets talked in hushed tones about the *U-47* raid as if it had only happened a few months earlier.

Presumably, some of this helped fuel Eddy Ross's curiosity about Nazi weaponry, much of which was considered vastly superior to the British at the outbreak of World War II. Eddy Ross was so intrigued that he began reading history and military books about Hitler and his brutal, murderous regime. Ross himself has never denied his interest in the history of the Nazi Party. However, he has always insisted he had no affinity whatsoever with Hitler's ideology.

By this time it was the mid-1980s. Social history had arrived on the scene and Nazi documentation had become available in large quantities. Some of it clearly fascinated Eddy Ross, who started to wonder how 'ordinary' Germans came to support Hitler's regime and why so few opposed it. He later said he treated Nazism like any other historical phenomenon without eschewing moral judgment and condemnation. Meanwhile, his appetite for reading up about the history of the Nazis continued to grow. As he admitted many years later, this meant that 'People automatically assume "racist". But I'm interested in all military history and in this case how such a small group could wield so much power.' Ross even later brushed off insinuations that he was a racist by telling one reporter: 'You couldn't print what I think about the British National Party.'

However, in the practical day-to-day world of Eddy Ross, there were duties to perform as a policeman and as a respected local pillar of society. There were two main police stations in the Orkneys; one based at Kirkwall and the other in the port town of Stromness. The outer North and South Isles were serviced by the Orkney Rural Beats Section, which also policed the communities of South Ronaldsay and Burray. These type of rural communities in Scotland continued to be considered safe places to live and work. Even so, during the 1980s, crime prevention became an increasingly important part of Eddy's duties as a local bobby. One former colleague explained, 'We were taught back then to literally keep the peace and try to prevent crimes before they were even committed by ensuring that any troublemakers in the community knew we'd come down heavily on them.'

Eddy's priorities at this time still mainly revolved around protecting livestock, securing farm machinery and preventing theft from fuel tanks. 'There were no big problems with juveniles back then in Kirkwall,' said a former colleague. Ross and other policemen were urged by their superior officers to use an old-fashioned, 'clip round the ear' policy when it came to petty troublemakers. The former colleague went on, 'Look, everyone round here knew everyone else back then. If you saw some kid throwing stones at the windows of a building, you'd chase them down and then give them a stern dressing-down and send them on their way. And most likely that kid's parents would be known to you anyway.'

But there were two distinct sides to Eddy Ross's character when it came to his policing skills. One co-worker explained, 'Despite our advice, Eddy could still be extremely old-fashioned and even petty with some people but others he was much more lenient with.'

None of this seems to have prevented Eddy Ross's career in the police from 'chugging along nicely', as they say in the Orkneys. Although some of his colleagues did find ex-army sergeant Eddy Ross a little intense. One fellow officer said, 'Eddy had this annoying habit of believing he was right about everything. Eddy Ross's self-belief was there for all to see, but it wasn't helping his career inside the police.'

At home, another son and a daughter eventually followed oldest child Michael. Eddy Ross adored it up on that blustery St Ola hillside overlooking Scapa Flow. He'd found a safe haven for himself and his family. Only about a dozen families lived within a mile of the Ross home. Eddy preferred it that way. No outside influences. No temptations. And more important than anything, he could control his family without any interference.

'Yeah, Eddy was rather controlling as a father and husband,' said one fellow officer, 'but on the other hand he provided his family with security and a nice home, which was more important than anything else. That meant a lot round these parts.'

And as ever, nobody seemed to bat an eyelid up in isolated St Ola when it came to Eddy's collection of guns. His closest neighbours respected Eddy because not only was he a policeman but he'd proved himself to be a 'true protector' when it came to his duties as a father and husband.

Eddy Ross's involvement with the Orkney Smallbore Association also continued despite his young children. At home he kept all his weapons safely under lock and key with strict orders to everyone in the family not to even attempt to open the cupboard containing his guns. The key to the cupboard was kept on a piece of string hanging around Eddy's neck. To the children that key must have represented authority. It gave Eddy all the power. The guns were his toys in a sense and he was not going to share them with anyone. On weekends, without fail, Eddy Ross would drive to the Orkney Smallbore Association range where he'd fire off live rounds with some of his oldest friends, many of whom were British Legion members he'd known since their childhoods together in the 1950s.

Eddy was renowned as a good shot but that was no big surprise since he'd been involved with guns from an early age, as well as being a trained marksman with the Black Watch. One gun-club member said, 'Eddy was a sharp-shooter, make no mistake about that and he was proud of his guns. During target practice, he always wanted to be the best. He was fiercely competitive. I remember one time when he was beaten by a youth who was the son of another member, Eddy was fuming. He didn't like losing to a mere kid. It annoyed the hell out of him.'

Back at the family home overlooking Scapa Flow, Ross the one-time Black Watch sergeant ran his household in his own inimitable way. He wasn't one to do many domestic chores. He left all that stuff to his hard-pressed wife Moira, who was also holding down a job as a nurse for cancer sufferers. At one stage in the late 1980s, Eddy Ross was transferred from Kirkwall to the Scottish mainland outpost of Kingussie, south of Inverness. The reasons behind this move have never been fully explained but it was quite a big upheaval for the family. But Kingussie was a sleepy little place, so none of Eddy's fears about the evils of 'urban communities' proved relevant. However, oldest son Michael in particular missed his friends back in the Kirkwall area and it is not clear whether Moira continued her job as a nurse in Kirkwall or quit while they were living in Kingussie. Ross assured his family it was only a short-term move and they'd soon be back in their beloved Orkneys and he proved true to his word. After less than a year, Eddy had persuaded his police bosses he should return to the family home overlooking Scapa Flow, which luckily they had decided to hang on to despite the move.

Eddy Ross had given up his membership of the British Legion when he was transferred to Kingussie and for a few years after the family's return to Kirkwall he allowed his membership to lapse. But eventually he rejoined the club. In many ways the house at St Ola had by then evolved into a perfect reflection of Eddy and Moira Ross as people. There was no fussy furniture or bright colours and a complete lack of cosy pillows on the sofa and chairs in the living room. Family photos were hung neatly on one wall above the sofa.

In the kitchen, no photos or notes were ever pinned to the fridge and there was only a handful of books on display with more, covering the Nazi Party and specialist gun publications, in a small side room that Eddy had turned into an office. Years later, Eddy described his home as containing many construction faults but with a view to die for. The lack of personal touches, apart from the family photos, was typical of the Ross family. No fuss. No drama. Just a solid family unit, or so it appeared to the outside world.

*Tjörn* was carpeted throughout to help deal with the cold drafts that came from the icy winds that swept up from Scapa Flow much of the year round. Sometimes the gusts were so strong they'd rattle the china knick-knacks on the fireplace in the Ross's living room. The wind even caused the big picture window that looked out over Scapa Flow to creak eerily. Those noises no doubt became part of the soundtrack to Michael Ross's early childhood.

As a former soldier, his father Eddy definitely saw most things in black-and-white terms. He considered himself to be brighter than most and this fuelled his very specific plan for his family's welfare and happiness. This worked fine during his children's early years and no doubt wife Moira was happy to let Eddy rule the roost. But Eddy Ross's expectation levels for his wife and children were high, to say the least. He particularly focused his attention on eldest son Michael, a chubby, reserved child who had always been anxious to please his father from an early age. Friends say that Michael had a constant smile on his face but it wasn't necessarily a genuine expression. He was just doing it to keep the adults happy.

Eddy Ross considered his first-born child to be a very special human being. He was determined to make Michael a strong, tough character. Many believe that Michael Ross was being nurtured into becoming a mirror image of his father, even from an early age.

One day in the mid-1980s, Eddy plonked his young son on his knee and encouraged him to help him clean his weapons on the family kitchen table. Gradually, Eddy took the gun apart so his son could study how each piece worked. Michael was a willing helper and Eddy had no doubt his son would one day be able to fire a weapon himself. All these close activities must have greatly helped father and son to bond. By the time Michael had reached eight years of age, his father had begun taking his him to the shooting range. So it was no surprise when Michael asked his father for a turn shooting.

Many adult members of the Orkney Smallbore Association brought their children with them on Saturday mornings to the range. But Eddy – by now secretary of the club – was particularly careful to only allow his young son to fire an air rifle. One former police colleague said, 'Eddy and Michael were like two peas out of the same pod back then. I remember they both had these very intense eyes that seemed to look right through you. It could be quite unnerving at times to see how in sync with each other they were.'

Another colleague said, 'Eddy was immensely proud of Michael from a very young age. It was typical father-and-son-type stuff. In fact, it was very touching in a way because Eddie wanted to involve Michael in every aspect of his life. A lot of fathers would never do that.'

Out on the firing range, the pair soon seemed to be attached at the hip. 'Michael would have this satisfying glint in his eyes when he hit the target and knew it would please his father, whom he would immediately turn towards for praise.'

At junior school in Kirkwall, though, Michael Ross seemed much more reserved. One of Michael's classmates recalled, 'Michael wasn't easy to talk to. He seemed a bit distant from the rest of us, even when he was about ten years old. It was only later I realised there was an arrogance to him, no doubt influenced by his father's opinions.'

On his beat, mainly in the Kirkwall area, PC Ross remained a disciplinarian. One officer recalled, 'Now with three children of his own, Eddy often stopped kids on their bikes to test their brakes and lights before forcing them to push their bikes home if there was anything wrong with them.'

Ross constantly encouraged his son Michael to physically challenge himself when it came to fitness. Michael never questioned his father's orders. He'd no doubt learned that taking orders was part of life, part of growing up. Likewise, Michael never questioned his father's extreme views about people like Adolf Hitler. Like a human sponge, young Michael sucked up all that information without ever questioning the wisdom of the most powerful person in his life at that time. And in the middle of all this, Michael, now almost twelve years of age, made it clear to a delighted Eddy that he had definite long-term plans to join the army and his first step in this direction was to join the local cadets.

Orkney's Army Cadet Force troops, of the Orkney and Shetland battery of the Lovat Scouts, was regarded as a superb training outfit for would-be soldiers. The original Lovat Scouts were a British Army unit first formed during the second Boer War in 1899 as a Scottish Highland yeomanry regiment of the British Army. They were the first known military unit to wear the camouflage ghillie suit, and in 1916 formally became the British army's first sniper unit, then known as sharpshooters. The unit served in World War I and II. Lovat Scouts were once described as half-wolf and half-jackrabbit by their German enemies. Their soldiers were well-practised in the arts of marksmanship, fieldcraft and military tactics. They were even trained to be phenomenal woodsmen so they could stay out in the field for days at a time. The Lovat Scouts' motto *'Je suis prest'* ('I am ready') summed up their attitude towards warfare.

Kirkwall's cadet corps was based near the sea's edge close to the town's harbour. It soon became clear to many of those at army cadet training that Michael Ross was streets ahead of most of the other youngsters when it came to knowledge of most aspects of army life. And naturally would-be soldiers like Michael were encouraged to show off their marksman skills at cadets. Eddy's decision to help his son learn to shoot from an early age had undoubtedly given his son an added advantage in the cadets and would eventually help him when he enlisted in the Black Watch regiment.

'Michael was way ahead of all his contemporaries in the cadet force. Most of them had never even been near a gun and here was this kid who seemed like a master marksman before he'd even become a teenager,' said one Kirkwall resident who knew the Ross family.

Eddy Ross's long-term strategy for his son was going exactly to plan.

# 4.

EDDY ROSS'S CAREER with the Black Watch regiment may have long since ended, but the rest of his family and many of his police colleagues knew he was still very emotionally attached to the army life and all the traditions and commemorations that came with it.

On Remembrance Sunday each year, Eddy and his family and hundreds of other local servicemen would attend Kirkwall's vast St Magnus Cathedral. Individual pipers would introduce the event with the traditional Scottish lament 'When The Battle's O'er', played at the end of conflict for centuries. For Michael Ross this must have been more music to add to the well-established soundtrack to his childhood, which had started with that strong wind whistling around their creaking home during severe winter storms.

Remembrance Sunday also showed Michael that he'd already been accepted into the fold when it came to the armed services. Eddy and his son jointly took part in a traditional parade that featured veterans plus local army and sea cadets, including Michael. Eddy and son would walk in an orderly fashion from Broad Street in the heart of Kirkwall to the cathedral, come rain or shine, each November. This was followed by a short service before a two-minute silence at 11 a.m., which was followed by another service inside the cathedral.

Many of these sort of experiences must have filled Michael Ross's mind during his childhood. Michael and later his younger brother Colin undoubtedly relished being part of a services' family. They must have been so proud to be marching alongside people who'd actually taken part in wars. It was almost as if both brothers were already part of the British armed forces.

A behavioural therapist said, 'These sort of activities would have had a profound effect on Michael. There's nothing negative about this at least on the surface. But I'd imagine Michael must have felt under intense pressure to prove to his father that he "enjoyed" these proceedings, whether he liked them or not.'

According to one of Michael Ross's classmates, 'Michael was swept up by all this army stuff being fed to him by his dad from a young age. While other kids were more into their toys, here was Michael being given a gun and being turned into a soldier and he was still pretty young. Sometimes we tried to loosen Michael up by teasing him a bit about all this soldier stuff and how it meant having to kill people. But he didn't like it and took it as an insult to his dad.' There was even one incident during which Michael Ross got into a fight with another boy as a result. 'That's when Michael started to become even more distant from many of us. It felt like he looked on us as the enemy in a way. His loyalty was clearly to his family and no one else. No doubt Eddy was proud of Michael but it felt like Michael was constantly on edge because he was having to prove himself to his father all the time.'

Meanwhile, Michael was starting to spend some of his time riding his bike fearlessly around a grim housing estate on the edge of Kirkwall. Kids in the area knew Michael Ross was a copper's son but they wanted to keep on his side, so they put up with him. Back in the warmth of the Ross family home up on that desolate hillside overlooking Scapa Flow, Eddy had his own strict set of rules that his children had to abide by. Television, for example, was a rare treat. There was one set in the living room, which was only switched on for a few hours a day at the most. Eddy and Moira were mildly disapproving of most programmes, except for special events such as the Queen's Christmas speech. No doubt, Eddy Ross reckoned the stunning bay of Scapa Flow and the bleak moors behind the family home contained much more entertainment value than television, despite the howling gusts of wind that constantly tore through the tiny community of St Ola.

Instead, Michael and his younger brother Colin were taught by Eddy to thrive in all weather conditions from a very early age. They needed to be able to cope with everything the gods could throw at them. Around the time Michael Ross turned thirteen, Eddy introduced a training routine that involved taking Michael (and later his younger brother Colin) by car into the moors at least five miles behind the family home in St Ola. Michael was encouraged to survive off grid, replicating being lost and having to find his own way home. Gradually, Eddy Ross increased the distance between Michael and the family home. The boy usually had nothing but a map, a compass and possibly a bottle of water. He'd then be told to get home before dark. In winter, the peat and heather received so much rain that anyone walking through it would get soaked to the skin.

One of Eddy Ross's colleagues said that Eddy believed 'it was character-building, although it seemed a bit strong to the rest of us. But in fairness he was the father and obviously he thought he was doing it in the interests of his son, so you couldn't pull him up on it.' Michael would then use all the skills he'd learned from his father, as well as techniques picked up from army cadet sessions, to battle through the elements to get home. No one knows what Michael's mother Moira thought of all this but one presumes that in both their minds it was a much healthier life than Michael sitting in front of a TV or computer game during his spare time. No one outside the family knows how Michael coped with this survival training. But there is no doubt that in Eddy Ross's mind it was all helping to shape his son's future career in the armed services.

The behavioural psychologist said, 'Today, this sort of parenting would be greatly frowned upon because it would be construed as a form of abandonment. That boy must have been terrified the first time his father did this. I guess he might have eventually understood how it would help him. But by then the damage might have already been done.' No doubt Eddy Ross had not forgotten the training exercises he faced in the freezing Scottish Highlands after joining the Black Watch as a rookie soldier in the late 1960s. With his son growing up fast, Ross was trying to replicate those sometimes brutal army training methods.

One Kirkwall resident who knew Eddy Ross well back then

in the late 1980s and early 1990s said, 'This was Eddy's way of toughening up his boy. He was obsessed with him joining the Black Watch and considered these sorts of exercises an ideal way to get Michael into shape for the future, literally.'

'It must have been tough on Michael,' said one resident of St Ola, where the Ross family lived, 'but he never complained. He just soaked it all up. In any case, he was in complete awe of their father. Maybe all Eddy's rules and regulations would help Michael and later his brother Colin to adjust to life in the armed services. But you have to wonder if it was worth a loss of their childhood from an early age.'

Another former resident said, 'It was all typical Eddy. He preferred to get Michael out on the fields than sitting on his backside at home glued to a small screen. Maybe Michael really didn't mind? But then again, he wasn't exactly given much choice in the matter.'

One police colleague said, 'Eddy was immensely proud of Michael (and later Colin) and openly told stories about how he'd drop him on the moors. Remember, this was nearly thirty years ago. No one back then was particularly bothered by Eddy being a disciplinarian. In any case, the Orkney Islands were and still are steeped in military history. This was just about a strict father keeping his two sons on the straight and narrow. We all tried to do that as parents.'

In some ways the Orkneys were a law unto themselves. People didn't interfere with the way others brought up their children. The Rosses lived in an isolated hill-top community where people knew to mind their own business, especially when it came to the activities of this tough, straight-talking policeman. Ross's gun collection had grown considerably. He now owned at least a dozen weapons including pistols, revolvers, rifles, and even a shotgun. And the only 'barrier' between his children and that deadly arsenal of weapons remained that key to the gun cupboard that hung on a piece of string around Eddy Ross's neck.

* * *

By the time Michael Ross enrolled in Kirkwall grammar school at the age of twelve, he must have appeared to the outside world as an exceptionally fit and well-adjusted child for his age. One old school friend said, 'Michael was an enigma. He seemed different from anyone else the moment he turned up at this school. We all knew he lived in St Ola and wondered how he had the energy to ride his bike up and down that huge hill, even in the worst winter weather. But then again many of the other kids from those isolated places like St Ola scattered around Kirkwall were just like Michael. Their character reflected the type of place they came from.'

Michael's new schoolmates didn't exactly welcome him with open arms. One later recalled, 'At first, Michael was shunned by quite a lot of us because he didn't seem to fit in with us. He didn't even have a favourite TV programme, for example, but we didn't realise he was hardly ever allowed to watch TV.'

Ross's heroes were real-life soldiers from the past like his own father. He was certainly able to talk to his classmates about Northern Ireland with great knowledge but none of them were particularly interested. Many of his classmates concluded that he would have preferred to be out on a shooting range or on an 'exercise' across the moors than in the classroom. One said, 'I remember Michael used to talk about hunting and shooting animals as if it was as normal as watching TV. That's when I started to realise that Michael was a very different animal from the rest of us.'

Michael Ross had also learned from his father to watch everything around him at all times. Being a professional soldier was all about self-protection, Eddy told his son. Once you were out in the field, your instincts and knowledge in that order were going to keep you alive. Nothing else. At the Orkney Smallbore Association range with his father, Michael no doubt relished every shot he took. He must have noticed the buzz that kicked in from the moment he picked up a real weapon. Many have said it's a unique combination of fear and anticipation. And pulling the trigger wasn't necessarily the most exciting bit.

The biggest thrill, many marksmen have recalled, was calmly entering the so-called killing zone, the 'place' from which you were about to fire your weapon. 'Knowing that you're in control. You are the one firing the gun and you know that a bullet is going to hit something very, very soon,' one retired army vet explained. 'It makes you feel almost invincible.' Inside his head, the shooter always knows he is playing judge, jury, executioner and even God almighty. They say that when that moment is reached the marksman is floating ten feet off the ground having gone 'into the zone'.

Michael Ross had already been taught by his father how to control the thought process at that very moment just before he squeezed the trigger. But he also had to learn how to keep his senses sharp and alert. He knew all about the art of accurate shooting. No doubt he adored the way adrenaline would pump through his veins every time he fired. That feeling of 'tuning' into every sound, sight, smell and movement around him. The smallest things would catch his eye. And Michael soon learned to pick up sounds that most people would not even notice. But then, Eddy Ross had been a professional soldier himself. Now he saw it as his duty to help his son. He believed he was simply doing his job as a father.

But as a thirteen-year-old schoolboy it wasn't so easy. In the USA, psychologists believe that being introduced to weapons at such an early age can lead to a gradual lack of appreciation of the obvious destructive qualities of a gun. All guns are, after all, killing machines. In fact, many so-called spree killers are brought up with guns all around them and this is said to disguise the reality of weapons and what they can do to people. One psychologist said, 'If you're encouraged to fire weapons from a young age it's doubly hard to step back from being in that so-called "killing zone". Guns become normal to you before you're even old enough to smoke cigarettes.'

And it's possible this was precisely what was happening to Michael Ross. His training as a marksman was so complete from such an early age that he'd long since learned never to jerk the trigger or abruptly clench his trigger-hand because it could cause the gun to move off target. He knew to place the pad of his index finger halfway between the tip and the first joint on the trigger without any movement. The actual squeeze of the trigger had to be made directly towards the rear of the gun. Any uneven pressure on it would shift the sight picture and cause the shot to go wide of the target. Then Michael would apply slow, steady pressure until the gun fired, while still being extremely careful not to slap or jerk the trigger. As the weapon was being fired, there was still a chance that powder flashing at the front of the cylinder might cause burns. Michael even knew how to keep his fingers away from the front of the trigger area.

*This schoolboy was now a highly trained marksman.*

In fairness to Eddy, he continued to be a stickler for gun safety throughout Michael's childhood. He'd long since told Michael about the safety catch that kept the trigger locked. He'd explained about the ejection ports on certain models over and over again. This would always ensure the gun was unloaded. Eddy had even shown Michael how to load weapons before he'd even fired one. Eddy had also pointed out how to place the stock of any gun so that it didn't recoil when fired.

Ultimately, these deadly weapons were now in the hands of a schoolboy. If he'd wanted to, Michael could have panned a gun around and shot at everyone near him on the firing range or maybe back at school. But he didn't and no one – including his own father – could have predicted how, despite all that expert training, a gun would one day change the entire course of Michael Ross's life.

# 5.

AT KIRKWALL GRAMMAR school, teachers and pupils recalled, Michael Ross was extremely quiet in class and not very attentive to what teachers were saying.

One classmate later said, 'He seemed a bit of daydreamer to us, unless he was talking about Scottish and army history. But there was this obvious inner toughness to him, though. You could see it in his eyes and I eventually found out to my cost that if he thought someone was doing him wrong then he'd soon let them know.'

When he was thirteen, Michael's army cadet unit went on a summer training camp to the mainland of Scotland where he was to earn himself almost legendary status. One cadet said, 'I have never forgotten what I witnessed at that camp. It all started when Michael stepped between one of his friends and a much bigger, older boy, who were having an argument.' The older boy immediately laughed in Michael Ross's face and then spat in his eye. 'That's when I noticed the expression on

Michael's face. It was challenging and fearless. He was almost smirking at this older, much bigger boy.' It seemed to many present that day that Michael Ross was showing admirable loyalty towards his friend and nothing and no one was going to stop him. That was when the older cadet punched Michael in the face really hard. 'And I mean hard,' the other cadet recalled. 'That punch should have knocked Michael flying but instead he just stood there without flinching a muscle.'

Then the same older boy punched Michael Ross even harder. 'But again, Michael still didn't move. It was quite incredible. No tears. No response. Just utter defiance on the part of Michael. It was as if he'd been trained to react that way. The weirdest thing of all is that Michael didn't cry. Later, I wondered if maybe this was something his father had taught him, so that he didn't lose his temper and could remain in control. But how could a thirteen-year-old have such self-control? Thinking about it later, I realised it wasn't a very healthy, normal response. But that older boy never went near Michael or his friend ever again after that.'

Other students who attended Kirkwall school and the army cadet troop meetings recall similar incidents involving Michael Ross. One said, 'It wasn't as if Michael was so big he could bully other kids because of his immense size. But he had this steely attitude which freaked out a lot of kids. It was a bit creepy I guess. None of us could work out how to handle Michael. Soon, most of us tried to tactfully avoid him because we sensed there was something lurking inside him if he was ever provoked.'

Ross proudly told classmates he couldn't wait to get in the army. 'It was as if he was already counting down the months and years to when he would enlist,' said one classmate.

By this time, many already knew about the gun skills taught by father Eddy and through Michael's army cadet training sessions. One classmate recalled, 'Some of us had dads who weren't around much and we felt kind of envious of Michael and his dad because we'd have loved to learn how to fire guns from an early age. It sounded like such fun to a thirteen-year-old.'

Children living in quiet rural areas like the Orkney Islands often joined the army cadets to gain access to a wide range of new activities. 'In some ways it was a bit like summer camp all year round,' one cadet explained. 'You gained a sense of comradeship as well but Michael already knew how to do most of the training. He led from the front at cadets but he didn't say much and we'd already heard a few strange stories about his antics at school, so some of us gave him a bit of a wide berth.'

While most of Michael Ross's fellow cadets looked forward to everything from kayaking to mountain biking, Michael Ross was fixated on improving his army survival skills as well as his shooting skills. 'The whole point of the cadets was to help develop these kids so they could build confidence and have a bit of fun,' said a fellow cadet, 'but Michael already had the skills of most adults and unfortunately fun didn't seem to be a word in his vocabulary.' Michael Ross was even earmarked as a potential future sniper for the British army. 'That says it all. He was being talked about as a professional killer from the age of thirteen. Mind you, it often felt as if Michael was five years older than he really was,' said a former cadet. 'His demeanour was that of a man-soldier not a young school kid who'd only just hit his teens.'

Back home, Michael Ross and his father continued to

bond closely, especially over their mutual love of guns. By this time Michael was permitted to fire off a wide range of Eddy's weapons at the association range but always under his father's strict supervision. Michael even got along well with the adult marksmen at the gun range. They treated him as an equal more than his teachers did at school. Michael was fascinated by some of his father's more colourful veteran friends. He lapped up their war stories and was immensely pride of his father's army exploits. In some ways, you could say that Eddy was living vicariously through his son. He no doubt missed the Black Watch regiment and couldn't wait for his oldest son to carry on the family tradition and join the regiment.

Meanwhile, the barren, windswept moors behind the family house at St Ola had turned into a playground of sorts for Eddy and Michael. By this time, Michael was being encouraged by his father to use a 12-bore shotgun to kill wildlife, often rabbits, which they'd track through the bracken for hours on end. For Eddy, hunting had always been a much more satisfying 'sport' than more traditional activities such as football and rugby. No doubt 'shootin' and huntin'' also suited Michael as well. And one presumes that by this time, Michael knew only too well about entering the co-called 'kill zone'. No doubt Eddy believed that getting Michael interested in guns and the army would help steer his son away from the more obvious teenage pursuits of sex, drugs and rock 'n' roll. And it was certainly true that as a thirteen-year-old, Michael Ross had few interests apart from what his father had taught him.

Had Eddy Ross become something of a mythical figure to his son? Eddy's life, past adventures with the Black Watch and even his obsession with guns must have all helped put him on a pedestal. But were Michael's expectations about his father unrealistic? If Eddy ever did upset the family in any way, was that a harder cross for Michael Ross to bear? Did he worship his father so much that there was only one direction he and his father could go in the long run? Sons are brought up to expect kindness and emotional support from their mothers, but the language they often use when talking about their fathers – hero, inspiration, role model – places a dreadful burden on real, flesh-and-blood men who cannot possibly live up to this high bar. Eddy seemed intent on pushing his son towards success and no doubt he would now say he only had his son's best interests at heart. Which may well have been true at the time. But many sons of fathers like Eddy Ross later admit that if they'd known the warts-and-all truth about their fathers then they might not have felt under so much pressure to live up to what they incorrectly perceived about them.

No one will ever know the full depth of the relationship between Eddy and Michael Ross but it seems unlikely they ever had a real opportunity to discover the real truth about each other. Eddy saw himself as the kind of man others should respect but was he being unrealistic wanting to achieve this goal? Was the pressure on Eddy so great that it turned him from being a caring father into an over-controlling parent?

Certainly, many people who knew Eddy Ross through his adult life were weary of him and his traditional, often rigid ways. But in fairness there were other occasions when they were also charmed by his sharp sense of humor. Was Eddy hiding something from his own childhood or adolescence that he didn't dare share with his son? Was it something he held so close to himself that he nurtured and strengthened it until he no longer knew whether the experiences were true or false?

Michael needed a hero to point the way to the future narrative his father demanded. But real life often doesn't work out that way.

Eddy Ross's reputation as a 'tough customer' policeman wasn't as consistent as it had once been. One self-confessed local Kirkwall tearaway later said, 'Knowing Michael got us a bit of a free pass when it came to Eddy. He'd tell us to scarper if we were up to no good rather than drag us back to the station, which would always end horribly because our parents would get called out. That was quite a surprise for someone like me. I was not exactly a good influence on Michael. But Eddy didn't seem to care about my background, even though he knew my old man and uncles were petty villains.' Eddy was undoubtedly confident that Michael could hold his own in such company. 'It's still strange, though, because you'd have thought Eddy would have looked on troublesome kids as a bad influence on his son.'

Ross's surprising attitude marked a big turning point in Michael's childhood. He was in effect being given a free pass to frequent the working-class streets of the sprawling Eastabist council estate, from where most of his toughest school friends came from. But even an obedient son like Michael Ross had to eventually show a rebellious side to his nature, although it appears he tried his hardest to hide it from his father. Like so many teenagers across the world, Michael Ross had begun to turn his bedroom at home into an individualistic shrine to things that his father might not like. He had just discovered thrash metal, in particular, the harsh sounds of pioneers Megadeth. Michael usually listened to them on earphones because he knew that the sounds would annoy his parents. Megadeth's music has been compared to napalm. Rapid-fire intensity that seemed to reflect the true anger of teenagers of that era.

No doubt, Michael Ross, like so many of his teenage contemporaries, adored losing himself in music. It was a form of escape from the drudgery of life, especially in a quiet place like St Ola. Megadeth lyrics would have soon begun resonating with him. The words often revolved around radical politics and death. At Michael Ross's school many pupils, especially boys, felt a connection to thrash, the high-energy, high-speed extension of heavy metal. Michael and his friends even became close disciples of Megadeth's leader, a wild character called Dave Mustaine, who said, 'We don't care about the future. We just want to be the most dangerous band on the planet.' Everyone in Megadeth had admitted to taking heroin. Interestingly, Michael Ross even put his own anti-drug sentiments aside when it came to Megadeth.

'This was Michael's way of being rebellious I guess,' said one school friend. 'With the TV banned most evenings by his father, he listened to Megadeth constantly in his bedroom, often when he was supposed to be doing his school homework.'

On the Orkneys, thrash metal at this time was by far the most popular brand of rock with anyone under the age of thirty. One Kirkwall resident explained, 'This is a desolate place. It's a harsh environment. The weather is often shit. No wonder the kids here turned to death metal in their droves. It spoke to them in many ways. Gave them hope and a chance to be rebellious because not many kids here were given much freedom.'

The release of Megadeth's 'Sweating Bullets' single from the band's 1993 album *Countdown To Extinction* had a particularly strong effect on Michael and many of his fellow metal fanatic friends. They adored the lyrics to the song that seems to speak to each and every one of them. When Megadeth announced plans for a European tour later that same year, the Orkney fans wanted to buy tickets for the Scottish leg of the tour but realised their parents would never allow them to go on the mainland. 'That was a pipe dream we all had,' said a school friend. 'At one stage some of us seriously contemplated sneaking onto the ferry, going to the concert and then sneaking back but it would have meant one overnight stay and we knew we'd never get away with it.'

There was another aspect to Megadeth that may have had a direct influence on young Michael Ross and in some ways legitimised Eddy and his more questionable interests at this time. The band had attracted Nazi and racists as followers and leader Mustaine seemed to fan the flames of such extreme attitudes through a tirade of anti-establishment rants that often sounded very right-wing. Down at the army cadet centre Michael attended every Wednesday, some of his fellow cadets also worshipped metal. This probably gave it an even bigger seal of approval to Michael. He even eventually had the courage to stick posters of the group on his bedroom wall. He also heard that many soldiers in the British and US services adored this brand of rock. For the first time in his life, Michael Ross had struck out and done something pretty 'normal' as a teenager.

His father had always said that loyalty to family and fellow soldiers was all that really mattered. But now Michael was definitely softening his attitude towards certain friends, many of whom lived on the rough Eastabist estate. He no doubt enjoyed the sense of belonging to a group of friends with no direct connection to the biggest influence in his life at that time – his father. One classmate said, 'I think Michael had become a bit of a rebel for the first time in his life. He seemed to turn into a more independent character than he'd ever been before.'

At last, Michael Ross felt free to do whatever he wanted.

# 6.

ON HIS FOURTEENTH birthday, in August 1992, Michael Ross was given a Raleigh Mustang mountain bike, which he immediately began using at high speed to pump up and down from his home in St Ola to Kirkwall. No doubt Michael found the journey much easier with this sophisticated new bike and its multiple gears.

This in turn gave him even more freedom when it came to spending time in Kirkwall, rather than at the family home on top of that isolated cliff overlooking Scapa Flow. Michael was spending more and more time with a small, select group of older school friends, most of whom lived on the sprawling Eastabist council estate close to the centre of Kirkwall. He also used his new bike to make the journey down for those 7 p.m. to 9.30 p.m. Orkney Cadet Force meetings on Wednesday evenings at the Lovat Scouts army reserve centre, on the outskirts of Kirkwall. Some Thursday evenings there was also a pipe and drums night to attend, when Eddy would often accompany his son.

But it was that sprawling Eastabist council estate that was starting to turn into a second home for an increasingly troubled Michael Ross. The estate's multi-layered concrete could not have been more different from the bleak, isolated location where Michael lived with his family. One of his oldest school friends said, 'Michael seemed more at ease with the harder characters on the estate than most of us. He fancied himself as a tough guy and you could already tell he wasn't scared of anyone.' He began spending an increasing amount of his time dressed in soldier-style clothing. He virtually always wore black combat boots to round off his outfits. 'Those boots told us everything,' a classmate explained. 'We knew Michael's dad was moulding him into a soldier and those boots seemed like the final piece in the jigsaw.'

According to one of Michael's first girlfriends, those boots were also used as a hiding place for weapons. She later recalled that Michael boasted he had a knife inside one and she concluded that was one of the main reasons why he wore them so often. There were also rumours that Michael sometimes kept a small pistol hidden in one boot, although that is less likely because of the size of such a weapon.

Michael had also developed other physical traits that seemed directly related to those training sessions with his father and his army cadet sessions. His classmates noticed he had got into the habit of hunching quite low when he was in the school playground. A friend said, 'Michael would always keep a low centre of gravity and then he'd turn and walk away from you in the middle of a conversation if he didn't agree with what you were saying. It was very disarming. Sometimes, I'd see him out on the fields around Kirkwall, running for miles on his own. I presumed it was part of an exercise routine but sometimes he'd stop suddenly, scan around in all directions as if he was looking for something and then carry on running even faster. It looked to me as if he was pretending to be in a warzone.'

In May 1993, Michael Ross went out on a supposed date with a girl he knew from the army cadets. They ended up walking to the main beach overlooking Scapa Flow, just a mile and a half away from Michael's family home. She was also fourteen. The girl was already aware that Michael Ross sometimes carried a knife either in a sheath on his hip or slipped down the inside of his platoon boots. She said that she leapt over a wall down to the beach and beckoned Michael to follow her but he refused and wouldn't explain, repeating, 'I'm not telling you. I'm not telling you.'

She said, 'He went on like this for ages and eventually told me he had one of his dad's pistols that he'd sneaked out of the house.' The girl said that Michael had told her that his father was away at the time. He then explained to the girl that he did not want to risk getting the pistol dirty in case his dad noticed. Michael never actually showed the girl the pistol or where he was hiding it. He also made a point of telling her he did not have any rounds for the weapon and insisted he had no intention of firing it that day anyway. The girl later said she was 'quite sure' she never actually saw him with any guns throughout their two-month relationship.

Kirkwall had some seven thousand inhabitants and to many visitors looked more like a Scandinavian community than a Scottish one. Its name came from the Norse 'Kirkjuvagr' ('Church Bay'), thanks to the foundation of the church of St Olaf in the city in the early-eleventh century. For the Norsemen at the end of the first millennium, Kirkwall was at the heart of a culture linking Scandinavia with Iceland, Shetland, the Western Isles, Argyll, parts of Ireland and the Isle of Man. For the seafaring Scandinavians, Kirkwall was not at the edge of the world but the very centre.

One of the biggest stories of recent Kirkwall revolved around the development of its harbour. By the early 1990s, Kirkwall's deep-water harbour was attracting more than seventy cruise ships each year to berth at the quayside. The visitors from those vessels said they felt safe and secure in Kirkwall's narrow streets and passageways but then there hadn't been a murder in Kirkwall for more than twenty years. One of the places most frequently visited by summer tourists, local residents and those cruise-ship passengers was the Mumtaz Indian restaurant, in Bridge Street, right in the heart of this stone-clad community. It was the city's only Indian restaurant at the time, although some locals had grumbled a tad when the previous traditional Orkney restaurant, the Ship Inn, was closed down to make way for the exotic, spicy food of India. The restaurant itself was slightly garishly decorated inside and out, which prompted more moans from the locals. But most regulars all agreed on one thing: the Mumtaz owner Moina Miah and his staff were charming and faultless and this was reflected by the number of regular customers.

Mr Miah lived with his family in a house nearby and the Bangladeshi waiters he hired all lived in a flat above the restaurant. Shamsuddin Mahmood was one of those happy-go-lucky waiters. A short holiday in the Orkney Islands in the previous summer of 1992 had convinced him to leave the home he shared with his brother in Southampton to take up the job in Kirkwall. Shamsuddin lived upstairs above the restaurant after arriving in 1993. Colleagues at the Mumtaz said Shamsuddin was warm, friendly and got on well with customers and staff.

Mahmood was one of seven brothers and four sisters who'd grown up in Bangladesh and he gained an economics degree, much to the delight of his family. There were high hopes Shamsuddin would become a lawyer like his older brother. Shamsuddin even had a sweetheart back in Bangladesh who was a medical student and the couple had talked about marrying in the near future. But there was pressure on him to do this before he'd settled into his chosen career. This then led to tensions that resulted in Shamsuddin rowing with friends over the relationship. That's when he moved from Bangladesh to the UK. Shamsuddin then disappointed his family by announcing he was giving up his law studies to work in Kirkwall.

Mahmoodquickly became a familiar figure out and about on the streets in the centre of Kirkwall. He surprised many, including his workmates, by the way he integrated with the locals. And of coursehewas easy to spot as there were virtually no brown-skinned residents in the whole of Orkney, let alone Kirkwall. As one local later noted, 'You couldn't miss him because he was a different colour from the rest of us. But many of us admired his determination to mix with the locals.'

However, there were other Kirkwall residents who were not so keen on Mahmood. As one later explained: 'There was talk in the town that Shamsuddin had turned up at a few after-hours-type parties after the restaurant had shut for the evening. I know some of the older residents were surprised because none of the other waiters mixed with the locals here.'

One night in the summer of 1993, Mahmood joined a group of twenty young people for a drink at a pub near the

Mumtaz. One of them said, '"Shamood", as we called him, turned up just before closing time and joined our group. We all knew him from the restaurant but his English was immaculate and he was extremely bright, so we really enjoyed his company. We were all in a merry mood but I remember noticing the faces on some of the older locals at the bar when we left the pub that night. They seemed to be sneering at us, particularly in the direction of Shamood. But I thought nothing of it at the time.'

A party of about twenty young people including Mahmood left the pub at 11.30 p.m. and headed round the corner to a flat lived in by one of the young women in the group. 'Shamood ended up entertaining two local women with amusing musical serenades, which we all found charming and harmless,' said one party guest.

Within such a tightly knit, isolated community as Kirkwall, there were sure to be some old-fashioned opinions on certain subjects, which more urban areas of the UK had long since settled. One resident later said, 'Racism was something rarely spoken about here but some of the older residents did seem to be a bit stuck in the stone age. I remember a black friend of mine coming over for a holiday around that time and he picked up on a racist reaction to him that he said he hadn't seen in London for years. I was shocked at the time and even tried to brush it off by accusing my friend of exaggerating.'

But the mumblings about 'people like Shamood' living in Kirkwall continued throughout 1993. Explained one islander, 'A lot of the older Orcadians used to proudly say that the islands were too isolated for any of the bad people to ever get to. But what they really meant was that it was off limits to black people and they wanted it to stay that way.' Mahmood told a couple of friends that he'd been racially abused in the street by a group of drunk youths on a number of occasions during that summer of 1993. But he brushed it off as 'old-fashioned' and refused to be put off Kirkwall although, in the late summer, he left his job and travelled back to stay with his brother in Southampton in the south of England. Yet, within weeks, he was trying to get his old job back in Kirkwall. At that time, there were no positions available. There was talk of Shamsuddin Mahmood having a secret girlfriend back in Kirkwall and that was why he was so desperate to return to the islands.

At home in St Ola, Michael Ross was expected to spend at least a couple of hours each weekday evening doing his homework, which gave him the perfect excuse to listen to Megadeth on his headphones. Michael may even have been starting to lose perspective on certain aspects of the reality of his life as he became more and more immersed in listening to Megadeth music, surrounded by Nazi regalia on the walls of his bedroom, undergoing strict army-style training sessions and hanging out with the rough crowd on the Eastabist. It would be alleged that Michael Ross's curiosity about the Nazis was further fuelled by another teenager he met a few months earlier at school who told him that the Orkneys would eventually disperse into a fragmented society once foreigners began showing up from the mainland demanding food, accommodation and work.

Just after Michael Ross's fifteenth birthday in August 1993, some classmates started to notice a distinct change in his character. One later said, 'He became even more distant from the rest of us in his school year. Michael seemed not to care about anything and it became much harder to have a conversation with him. I'd often catch him sneering at the rest of us, as if he had some great big secret he would never share with us. It was quite unnerving but then again he wasn't unique. We were teenagers after all.' Around this time, Ross also became the go-to person when it came to settling feuds. 'Michael said he'd always happily sort out anyone whom he felt was bulling any of us, even though in some ways he was the bully, not them and I wondered if he was offering this "service" just to ingratiate himself with us.'

By late 1993, Ross had clearly become the self-proclaimed protector of a number of boys and girls at Kirkwall school who found themselves threatened by other pupils. One student said, 'Many of us had heard about how he soaked up physical punishment from older boys when he was younger but now it seemed to be his turn to hit back.' Some classmates believed he was 'empowered' by carrying a weapon in those ever-present combat boots. All knew of his skill with guns and how he was often out shooting with his father. In a sense, Ross was developing into a mythical, mobster-type character, striking fear into many and getting himself a reputation as someone few would dare challenge.

In his head, Ross must have been feeling invincible whenever he wasn't at home, where he was the dutiful son learning from a knowledgeable, disciplinarian father. Down on the Eastabist estate, he was a different animal: other teenagers looked up to him, they feared him, and he was hanging out with a posse of youths who ruled the streets of the estate. One member later said, 'Michael was a tough nut. He earned a place with our group and we looked on him as our secret weapon, someone we could wind up and send out to sort out people who had crossed us.'

By this time, Ross was allegedly consuming alcohol but he refused point-blank to go near drugs, which met with his disapproval. One classmate explained: 'Michael often dismissed a lot of the kids at the school as "druggies". I think he even beat a couple of boys up when they tried to sell drugs to one of his classmates.'

One of his friends on the estate said, 'One time Michael went after completely the wrong kid who'd been incorrectly identified as having stolen another boy's watch. Michael planned it all like a military operation, then beat the boy to a pulp only to find out he hadn't done it.' This alleged incident had the effect of terrifying even more of Michael's classmates, which in turn gave him more power and influence at school and on the estate. A couple of girls in his year even decided to use him to deter boys who were pestering them for sex.

As a student of the time said, 'Michael seemed to thrive on the fear and trepidation everyone felt about him by this time.' But there was another, even more chilling factor when it came to Ross's power and influence at school. Another classmate said, 'Some us genuinely feared that Michael might turn up at the school with a gun and start shooting everyone if we upset him.' There were rumours at Kirkwall school that Michael had sometimes brought a gun with him to the classroom. It should be pointed out that there was never any concrete evidence of this, 'but just knowing he had access to those guns or other weapons was enough to scare a lot of kids,' said a pupil. Naturally, Michael Ross did very little to dispel those rumours. The same classmate later said, 'I think he enjoyed seeing the look of fear on kids' faces whenever they sensed they were about to have a run-in with Michael.'

But Ross's hard-man status did have one unlikely spin-off.

# THE SNIPER'S STORY

A fellow student said, 'Michael became increasingly popular with girls. None of these relationships seemed to last long but many girls liked his bad-boy image.' Ross became friendly with a girl he met at army cadet sessions on Wednesday evenings. She later recalled how Michael one day turned to her and said, 'Blacks should be shot and guns put to their heads.' She dismissed Michael's outburst as 'showing off to an audience', but she never forgot the venom with which he said those words.

It was clear that by this time Michael Ross had developed two distinct sides to his character. Regular training exercises, shooting on the range with his father and weekly cadet sessions still took up much of his time when he wasn't cycling back and forth to the Eastabist. But that estate now represented another world to Michael Ross in many ways. His new, closely knit group of older friends were feral in the sense that they wandered around Kirkwall on their own from a relatively young age.

As a result, many of them were drinking alcohol, which they'd consume on the grasslands dotted around the estate or down one of the numerous alleyways near the centre of Kirkwall. Ross and others were sometimes seen staggering around the narrow streets and alleyways of the town. No one knows if Eddy Ross had any inkling that his oldest son was drinking heavily with a crowd of older youths. The key to Michael's new world on the sprawling council estate was his bicycle. It enabled him to ride at high speed up and down from St Ola whenever he wanted to. As one friend from Eastabist said, 'He used to thrash that bike up and down from St Ola all the time. Some days he'd come down to town early afternoon, hang out with us, then go back to St Ola for tea before rolling back down the hill early evening. He said it kept him fit and maybe that's why Eddy didn't mind. But I think Michael was starting to feel happier with his mates than being at home.'

\* \* \*

In Southampton at his brother's house, former Mumtaz waiter Shamsuddin Mahmood continued pressing the owner of the Kirkwall restaurant for his old job. In April 1994, his wish was finally granted and he returned to live in Kirkwall and was made manager of the restaurant. Many customers were delighted to see the return of Mahmood. As one later said, 'He was a charming guy. Always smiling. Always helpful and he'd integrated so well with the locals.' There were even fresh rumours that Shamsuddin had a secret sweetheart on the Orkneys. One of his Kirkwall friends said, 'We never knew for sure because he wouldn't say but I think there was a girlfriend here.'

Another resident, who'd attended a couple of parties with Mahmood, said that the young man, who was also known as 'Shamol', once again found himself facing vicious verbal racial attacks from groups of local youths in the town centre: 'When we were all out as a group in Kirkwall town centre with Shamol, we did sometimes get some comments from other more ignorant locals as they walked past us. There were also a couple of groups of teenage kids who shouted abuse at Shamol and us for being with him. It was very unpleasant but Shamol didn't seem bothered and just laughed it off.'

Some have speculated that by having a relationship with a local girl, Mahmood may have been infuriating local racists. But this has never been properly established. It was even later claimed that there another reason for his return to Kirkwall. One restaurant regular later said she had overheard a customer ask Shamsuddin Mahmood why he was back in the Orkneys and he'd responded: 'I have to be here.'

By Easter 1994, the Mumtaz restaurant had built up a large customer base and was managing to attract at least thirty customers each night of the week. Many of those came between 5 p.m. and 8 p.m. and tended to be families on special nights out or older residents. The 'late crowd', as staff called those customers who came after 8.30 p.m., were a different type altogether. They were often much younger locals dining at the Mumtaz after a tankful of beers in the local pubs. New manager Mahmood and his fellow Bangadeshi worker, Khukon Uddin, had learned to be wary of these customers, some of whom would mutter derogatory racist terms if their food or beers did not turn up quickly. Mahmood always tried to have a smile on his face and chose to completely ignore the remarks, according to those who knew him.

He even told one friend he appreciated why the locals were so anti-strangers on the islands. 'Shamol understood Orcadians. He recognised that we were a bunch of loner types and this brought with it a lot of ignorance on certain levels,' said one of Mahmood's friends in Kirkwall. Mahmood defended Orcadians to his friends and fellow staff members at the Mumtaz by saying they were just shy. 'Typically, Shamol chose not to consider the bad aspects of some of the people round here.'

But the drunken revellers who swamped the narrow streets and alleyways at weekends after the pubs closed were sometimes a lot more than just shy. Mahmood's friend said, 'Everyone who comes to Kirkwall is always surprised by the amount of drunks in the town centre late at night, especially at weekends. We used to blame it on the number of pubs but it was, and still is, also about the stubborn mentality of a certain section of the population. And then of course there is the boredom suffered by many of the younger people here. There just isn't much to do here except drink.'

The local youth community centre was a hub of sorts for teenagers frequenting the town centre area. But it only stayed open until 7 p.m. Many teenagers then turned to alcohol, buying in local shops or going into pubs that at that time tended to turn a blind eye to alcohol being drunk underage. Was all this excessive consumption of alcohol blurring the lines between thoughtless drunken jibes and vicious, all-out racism?

# 7.

BY THE LATE spring of 1994, Michael Ross was fifteen-and-a-half and had been on at least a dozen dates with girls in the Kirkwall area over the previous year.

'His reputation as the original bad boy continued to attract girls,' said a classmate. 'Stories of how he sorted out other kids who crossed him seemed to make some girls more attracted to Michael and his broody looks.' Some of those girls later described him as shy and brooding and prone to making blunt statements about race and drug users. He seemed to find it hard to communicate with the opposite sex on a normal level and these relationships quickly fizzled out as the girls got bored with his company.

They also found Ross's straight dress sense hard to comprehend. He might have been a diehard Megadeth fan, but he certainly didn't copy the way his idols dressed. He either went in for the quasi-military look or otherwise sported drab tracksuits and T-shirts, both styles usually rounded off with his combat boots. 'None of us ever dared confronted Michael about it, but those boots seemed so out of place compared to the trainers we all wore,' said one fellow pupil. 'I think Michael reckoned they made him look harder. Certainly, the boots scared us because they could cause some real damage if he decided to kick the shit out of anyone.' And by the late spring of 1994, fresh rumours began circulating Kirkwall grammar school that Michael was once again hiding a small gun inside those same combat boots. There were also stories on the Eastabist estate that Michael Ross had actually fired a real gun at a wooden target in one friend's back garden. Naturally, this gossip did Michael's growing reputation as the school hard man no harm whatsoever.

Back up the big hill at his home *Tjörn*, in windswept St Ola, Michael had started a collection of items he called his 'army stuff'. This included balaclavas, hoods and other regalia that he one day believed he might need to wear to 'sort out' his enemies in Kirkwall. Ross even later claimed his father Eddy had a similar collection, including balaclavas. Meanwhile, in his bedroom, Michael Ross continued listening round-the-clock to Megadeth tracks on his earphones with a tacit agreement from his parents that they would not enter his bedroom without knocking.

As with most teenagers across the world, Michael's bedroom had by this time evolved into his own private, safe haven. It's impossible now to know precisely what was going through Ross's mind at this time, but it most likely centred around violence and retribution combined with plans to become a professional soldier. Michael knew from his training sessions with his father and the army cadets that battles were often won by those with the best plans and preparation.

Eddy Ross has never disclosed whether he knew his son was in danger of going off the rails at this time. But there were small hints that their close bond may have taken a few knocks during the late spring of 1994. No doubt the older Ross tried to stay close to Michael by continually encouraging him to work towards a career in the army. All Eddy really wanted to do was to ensure his son avoided the pitfalls that are a threat to many children's teenage years. Focus was imperative and Michael certainly had bucketloads of that.

School no doubt felt like a big waste of time with Michael's other plans. He already knew what he wanted to do in the world. Now he was counting down to the moment when he would get into the army and be able to shoot at all his enemies legally. Schoolmates later said that during the late spring of 1994, the fifteen-year-old had become even more distant from most of his contemporaries while spending a lot of his time with that older, rougher crowd on the estate. Around this time, Eddy presented his son with a gift, a decommissioned sub-machine-gun. Michael adored the weapon so much he immediately hung it over his bed on the walls covered with Megadeth posters and a Nazi propaganda poster with a swastika adorning it. Third Reich regalia had become normalised for him to a certain degree through Eddy's interest in right-wing extremist literature. Under Michael's bed in a plastic bag sat the black balaclava with holes for the eyes and mouth and a few other items that might one day come in handy.

His classmates noticed that he constantly scribbled swastika emblems on his school exercise books. It was not clear if any of his teachers or fellow pupils voiced their objections but his interest in Hitler and the Nazis seemed to be growing.

At army cadet sessions, Ross now had the rank of corporal and he was so proud of this that he even drew two chevrons for corporal and the word Ross on all his exercise books at school. The 'o' of 'Ross' had been drawn with a swastika inside it, while the 'ss' of the name resembled the Nazi SS lightning-bolts logo – SS short for *Schutzstaffel*, the feared Nazi paramilitary organisation. Also in the notebook was a Scottish Saltire flag, inscribed with the caption 'Death to the English' and a banner on the same page reading 'Death cures all'. Eddy Ross pointed out that scribbling swastikas on school books had been commonplace when he was a child in the '50s and early '60s. But by 1994, such emblems of right-wing extremism were not so well known to most children.

Michael and his father weren't the only Orcadian citizens with an interest in right-wing fanaticism. One of Michael's former classmates recalled, 'Some of the parents of kids at the school were pretty far right in their beliefs. They saw the mainland as a den of vice and genuinely believed that preventing "bad people" from coming to the islands required some pretty extreme measures. Many of the people with these sort of beliefs seemed to come from services backgrounds and a lot of them lived on the Eastabist estate. My family thought the British Legion clubhouse was a hotbed for these sort of characters. It's obvious their children would have been deeply influenced by those attitudes.'

Eddy Ross didn't hide his interest in Hitler and the Nazi Party – but how much of this rubbed off on his family? Ross himself later tried to laugh off any effect this might have had on his eldest son by saying, 'Rabbit shooting, that was about the level of his politics. A racist? Rubbish. I don't think so. Michael never did much with books at all. I never talked to him about these things. It was reading material for my own consumption.'No doubt some of his son's classmates still envied the close bond Michael had with his father. But did Michael truly appreciated how lucky he was to have such a close relationship with his dad?

As one pupil said, 'A lot of us hardly ever saw much of our dads, if we even had one. But Michael's dad was not only a local policeman but he was also encouraging his son to fire guns on a range and helping shape his future career. A lot of us would have given anything to have that sort of dad.'

In the middle of May, Ross was out riding his bike through the estate when he bumped into a teenage girl he'd once dated and was shocked to see that she had cuts and bruises on her face. The girl showed Ross bruises on her ribs and her back and blamed all the injuries on a new boyfriend. But she never told Ross why the boy had beaten her up. Ross became so incensed by what he saw that he decided to 'get' the girl's assailant to 'teach him a lesson.' Ross was hoping to rekindle the relationship because they'd only gone out together for about seven weeks and he was desperate to see her again. He spent the next few days planning his attack in minute detail. He even carried out a reconnaissance of the area where her assailant lived and the boy's route to school from his home. Ross established that his target would be walking through an area called Papdale Woods, a small cluster of trees in the middle of the estate where Michael was spending so much of his time. Michael informed the girl that it was the perfect location for him to sort out the other boy.

The Orkney islands has long been known for its lack of trees and Papdale Woods was a well-known beauty spot, renowned as an oasis of tranquility in the middle of the urban community. 'We call it one of Kirkwall's rare natural treasures,' one resident said. The woods themselves consisted of tightly packed trees, originally planted two hundred years earlier by a landowner who'd built a house and then pronounced himself lord of the manor.

At around 3 p.m. on 19 May 1994, Michael Ross dropped his beloved Raleigh bicycle off at his grandmother's house near Papdale Woods because he didn't want to risk it being damaged if his 'revenge mission' went wrong in any way. A few minutes later, Ross arrived at the woods, took out a balaclava and a hooded sweatshirt from his backpack and changed into his 'combat uniform'. Then he began rehearsing how he would assault the other boy in a series of carefully planned movements. He had learned from cadet sessions and his father that preparations were key to the success of such an 'operation'. About a hundred yards away in the back garden of a house on the Eastabist estate, a mother and her teenage daughter noticed a hooded figure 'stalking' through the wood, crouching and then running around trees and bushes as if on a training exercise. They watched Ross for at least half an hour carrying out his 'manoeuvres' and he was also spotted by an assortment of other children on their way home from school.

As the wind swept up from the harbour side of Kirkwall that afternoon, it made the trees rustle so noisily that the sounds of Michael's movements and grunting noises were drowned out to a certain extent. However, some witnesses later said they heard Michael muttering to himself as if he was giving himself a running commentary on his own plans. The trees in Papworth Woods were so close together that it made full visibility very hard for the mother and daughter watching from their garden. The trees themselves also prevented much light reaching the ground so the soil underfoot was uneven and covered in mosses, ferns and lichens, as well as a smattering of grasses and shrubs. The mother and daughter later said the figure was wearing a dark blue, woolly jumper with a hood over his head. It was a very warm day so this had caught their attention in particular. The mother also noticed that the figure seemed 'edgy' and that he kept looking all around as if trying to make sure no one was watching him. He was also ducking and swerving between the trees in the wood. They were transfixed by what they saw. Others witnesses later said they noticed that the hooded person seemed to have a wooden box with him, as well as his backpack. Later it was claimed this may have contained a gun of some sort. The mother and daughter became so concerned one of them grabbed some binoculars from inside their home so they could watch the figure more closely. Other witnesses later recalled that the person was so wrapped up in what he was doing that he didn't seem to notice he was being watched.

Ross has always maintained he was in Papdale Woods that afternoon preparing himself to ambush that other boy who'd been due to walk past the wood at that time. But to the watching mother and daughter and other eyewitnesses, Michael seemed to be preparing for something much more significant. The mother later said, 'At one stage he had the mask over his face. Other kids were walking home from school at this time and I was worried for their safety.'

Michael Ross continued his exercises, occasionally crouching down next to a wall that ran alongside the side of a road. A few minutes later the same woman's daughter and a school friend walked right past the masked figure in the woods. They were startled when he suddenly leapt over the wall, dived behind a tree and began taking his hooded top off. He had another balaclava on underneath it and removed that as well, so they could see his face clearly. In the wood, Ross put the top and balaclava in his back pack. Underneath he was wearing a light-coloured jumper with a pattern along the bottom hem.

At 3.45 p.m., half an hour after he'd first entered the woods, Ross walked calmly out of the area and up the road towards a hostel where he believed his target lived but he didn't find him. A few minutes later, Ross casually popped into the garden of his grandmother's nearby house, grabbed his bicycle and headed off back up that big hill to St Ola.

The mother and daughter eyewitnesses later described the man as having very short, fair hair and a tanned complexion and he seemed to be about five foot and seven inches tall. He appeared nervous and in his early twenties. Ross later claimed he dropped his revenge mission plans against the other boy before the boy had even realised he was Michael's intended target. Ross said, 'I did not have any weapons on me when I was in the woods and I was just going to punch him if I got him.' Whatever the truth of the matter, something was eating away at Ross and he was becoming increasingly obsessive and paranoid.

Some of his contemporaries later said that Ross had been devastated when the girl who was later beaten up by that other boy had ditched him after a few weeks and that had sent him hurtling towards an emotional train crash. It seems that Ross had spent so much of his spare time training with his father and at the army cadets that he'd never given much thought to rejection by a girl and now he was suffering from what some believe may have been a broken heart. Classmates later insisted that Ross was not fully connected with his own feelings and found it harder than most to control his emotions of love and hate. He had wanted to rekindle the relationship with that girl but the only way he knew how was through violence. Ross later insisted he had never carried out an attack like this before. But he had, by this time, developed a hair-trigger temper. One of his classmates later recalled: 'Michael seemed to be on edge all the time. He was like a bomb waiting to explode.'

At the Mumtaz restaurant, in the centre of Kirkwall, friendly new manager Mahmood was finding it harder to deal with youths shouting racist insults at him and his staff than he had the previous year. A number of regular customers at the Mumtaz later gave statements expressing varying degrees of concern about Mahmood's demeanour at the restaurant towards the second half of May 1994. Many claimed his mood was more morose compared to his previous talkative, charming manner. One customer said that he was even quite gruff with customers. Another regular who'd got to know Mahmood well during his first stint at the Mumtaz in 1993 said, 'He became much more withdrawn, didn't want to acknowledge anyone.' A customer who ate at the restaurant towards the end of May 1994 said, 'He seemed low and was not his usual, happy self . . . he seemed preoccupied, as if he had something on his mind.'

Another Mumtaz customer noticed that Shamsuddin Mahmood kept 'nervously peering above the menu' towards the door of the restaurant. That same customer later recalled: 'When he was writing out the "chitty" for my order, he looked up four or five times towards the door. He didn't seem at ease.'

## THE SNIPER'S STORY

It was later alleged that Mahmood had clashed with some people in the town who did not like the way he was socialising with the locals. One Kirkwall resident later said, 'If that is the case then it's shaming for Kirkwall and the Orkneys in general and shows just what a backward, bigoted society we live in.' Whatever the truth of the matter, an underlying tone of hatred was growing in the centre of Kirkwall and it was pointed in the direction of Shamsuddin Mahmood.

Part Two

# The Kill

'The Sniper must not be
susceptible to emotions
such as anxiety and
remorse.'
— Craig Roberts, author
and former sniper

# 8.

ON 31 MAY 1994, a Tuesday, twelve days after the incident in Papdale Woods, a number of youths turned up drunk for a meal at the Mumtaz restaurant and seemed determined to cause trouble. Shamsuddin Mahmood and his colleague Khukon Uddin eventually had to ask the youths to leave the premises. As Mahmood escorted the troublemakers outside, two other youths appeared on the pavement outside the restaurant.

They immediately began taunting Shamsuddin about his colour. Then, as one youth was about to walk away, he turned and aggressively stared right into Shamsuddin's face. 'I'm gonna shoot you,' he said before stumbling up the narrow lane in front of the restaurant. One witness later said the youth repeated the shooting warning three times and smiled.

The next morning islander Norman Johnston saw two men acting suspiciously down at the pier in Kirkwall. They were in a Ford Orion car driving up and down the wrong way before one got out and stared up the street where the Mumutaz restaurant was located. Johnston recalled, 'The car had silver Hammerite paintwork. It was very distinctive, a terrible paint job. One of them kept looking up the street where the restaurant was. I went to the chip shop. He was still there when I came back. Tall, with a shaved head, tanned and wearing an army-type shirt. He was looking about, and then sat in the car and it drove away.'

Later that same day, Michael Ross attended the army cadet centre at Weyland, near Kirkwall, but he was clearly on edge and soon became involved in an altercation with another cadet while the pair were doing drill together. The other boy allegedly told Ross to 'fuck off' when Michael pulled rank and ordered him to work harder at the drill. Ross himself later admitted he was infuriated by the other boy who he considered to be insubordinate because Ross was a corporal and the other boy was a private. The clash ate away at Michael Ross for the remainder of that cadet training session. As the cadets left later that evening, Ross grabbed the other boy and punched him in the face. The other boy did not retaliate.

Ross's father Eddy attended the cadet hall that evening and drove Michael and all the other cadets home in the minibus as he often did in his capacity as a training officer. But some have since asked why Eddy felt the need to drive his sons around that particular night. Was Eddy worried about what might happen to Michael after that fight at the cadet meeting?

On the morning of 2 June, Ross and his brother Colin were both off school the entire day because they were supposed to be studying their prep work at home. At 10 a.m., Eddy Ross used the cadet van – which it was alleged he parked at the family house overnight – to take Michael and Colin into Kirkwall with the express intention of then returning the van to the cadets' hall in town, where he had left his car the previous evening. Ross himself told this author in March 2019 that he 'couldn't recall' whether or not he had kept the scout van overnight. He said, 'It was a long time ago. I really can't remember whether I parked it at home that night or not.'

At Kirkwall grammar school that same morning, there were already rumours about how Michael Ross had punched the boy at army cadets the previous evening. One classmate later said, 'The boy had insisted it was an unprovoked attack and he never told Michael to fuck off. Some were shocked by what had happened and said that Michael was out of control. Michael seemed to be in a bad place at this time. Anyone who did anything to him was likely to get punched in the face, which was why most of us steered clear of him.'

In Kirkwall town centre, Eddy Ross dropped his two sons off outside the Territorial Army Centre and they both walked together through the narrow lanes and streets into the centre of town. At about 12 p.m., Michael Ross bought himself a roll at a shop called Cumming & Spence and then both brothers walked to the community centre, near the town hall. They stayed in the area that afternoon, returning to the centre of town to look in various shops. Then, at about 4 p.m., Ross met his father outside Woolworths and got a lift home. His brother Colin stayed in town.

Those who were out and about in Kirkwall that warm summer's evening later recalled that the smell of newly mown hay mingled with the sounds and smells from the busy pier district wafting pleasantly through the centre of town. It seemed like a normal day.

Ross arrived home with his father at about 6 p.m. and went straight to his bedroom to listen to Megadeth and study his homework before emerging for an early dinner with his parents. He returned to his bedroom, where he packed his rucksack with items including his balaclava. He also put on a multi-coloured blue, orange yellow and black jacket in case it rained. He was wearing jeans and his beloved combat boots.

Three hundred miles south on the Mull of Kintyre, at about the same time Michael Ross got home, an RAF Chinook helicopter crashed into a hillside killing all twenty-five passengers and four crew on board. As a result, all emergency services in the Highlands rushed to the scene, leaving the rest of the region uncovered for the remainder of the evening. Among the passengers on that helicopter had been almost all the UK's senior Northern Ireland intelligence experts. The accident went on to hold the distinction of being the worst peacetime disaster to have been suffered by the RAF.

At around 6.30 p.m., Ross jumped on to his bicycle and headed back down the hill to Kirkwall, listening to yet more Megadeth on his earphones as he pumped furiously on the pedals to get him into town as quickly as possible. Ross was in 'mission mode', it seems. He had plans for that evening. Ross later claimed he cycled around Eastabist estate. Ross knew the area so well that he'd even learned all the street names off by heart. Ross said he then met some friends in an area called Meadows where many of those in his posse of older friends lived. Just a short distance up the road resided former marine James Spence, a friend of Eddy, who would eventually emerge as a pivotal figure in the future of both Rosses. Ross later claimed that he spoke to a girl and boy on the estate about how he'd punched the boy the previous evening at cadets and they told him how everyone at school had been talking about it. Ross said one of his friends asked to see his grazed knuckles.

Whatever the truth about Michael's movements that evening there seems little doubt he was on some kind of adrenaline high because those who encountered him said that his eyes seemed glazed and he was having trouble listening to anything being said to him. Less than half a mile away, in the centre of Kirkwall, waitress Marion Faws and her manager Shamsuddin Mahmood had been at the Mumtaz since around 4.30 p.m., opening for the early shift of customers. Marion had worked at restaurants on the same site for many years. By about 6.45 p.m. she and Mahmood had cleared the first sitting and were waiting for another surge.

At this time, Ross was cycling around the Eastabist, incensed, having being told that the boy he hit the previous evening had considered reporting him to the police for the attack. Michael was irritated that anybody would even dare threaten to 'grass' him up.

Less than five minute's cycle ride away, a man entered the Kiln Corner public toilets in the centre of Kirkwall. He immediately locked himself in a cubicle and changed into clothes that were in a back pack. The man's breathing was heavy and each time he put on a new item his hands and arms smashed against the walls of the narrow cubicle. Once he'd changed, the man stopped and listened for a few seconds to make sure no one else was in the toilet before unlocking the door. He then emerged and headed straight for the exit, shoulders down, knowing precisely where he was heading. One hundred yards away Mahmood and Flaws greeted between fifteen and twenty new customers, including local businessman Donald Glue, his wife and two young daughters. Outside, the summer sunshine was still beating down on the narrow lane as a warm, rippling breeze blew gently in from the nearby sea.

# 9.

SHAMSUDDIN MAHMOOD HAD just started taking an order for food from the Glue family when Marion Flaws saw a man walk in the Mumtaz wearing a dark balaclava with two small slits for the eyes. He was holding a gun.

Marion Flaws later recalled, 'He moved very quickly towards the Glue family sitting at the far end as Shamsuddin wrote down their food order. I remember thinking if he was a robber his timing was bad because the restaurant takings had not been good that day.'

Mahmood looked up and smiled momentarily as the masked man walked briskly towards him. Then the man raised his weapon. Donald Glue turned to him and asked, 'What the hell are you doing?' Mr Glue later said, 'I thought it was some kind of joke – that it was going to be a water pistol sprayed on the waiter's face.'

Before Mahmood had time to react, the man in the balaclava leaned across Mr Glue's seven-year-old daughter Sarah and squeezed the trigger of the gun tightly grasped in his hand. The 9mm bullet shot at point blank range into the face of Shamsuddin Mahmood pierced his right eye and travelled through him before exiting his shoulder and embedding itself in the wall. An empty bullet casing bounced in slow motion onto the carpet.

One witness later described the shooter's actions: 'He looked very calm, as if he had rehearsed it all and knew exactly what he was doing.'

Donald Glue later recalled, 'A split second after he fired, I thought, Christ, he's going to turn it on the kids. The whole thing cannot have lasted more than ten seconds.'

Part of the left side of Mahmood's head fell on the table where the Glue family were sitting. Pieces of his flesh splattered onto the face of Mr Glue's daughter. As the victim's body hit the floor, an eerie silence enveloped the restaurant. Meanwhile the killer reached the door, still holding the gun. He threatened no one else and said not one word. Then he opened the door and left.

This brutal, seemingly senseless act understandably left many customers screaming and panicking. Outside, the shooter darted down the lane towards an alleyway. Moments later, Mr Glue and his brother-in-law, who was at another table, flung open the door to the restaurant in pursuit of the killer. They shouted after him but then stopped just as the man went down the alleyway off the main lane. 'We were scared he might shoot at us so we stopped following him,' Mr Glue said.

Mahmood's colleague Khukon Uddin had been watching a video in a room above the restaurant at the time of the killing. 'I came down and saw him lying on the ground and bleeding from terrible head wounds,' he later said. 'All I could think of was that this was a racial attack by someone who didn't like the colour of our skin.'

In the restaurant, Mr Glue returned to his table to find everyone else looking down at the corpse of someone they had all been speaking to just moments earlier. Young Sarah broke down in tears as she recalled the horrifying scene later. She said, 'When the gun went off, I wasn't aware of what had happened. It then became obvious.'

With Mahmood dying on the floor and other people trying to help him, one customer took off their jacket and put it under his head. Then his body was covered with another jacket in an attempt to keep him warm. With some customers screaming and others stunned into silence, Marion Flaws ushered them to the other end of the restaurant. One customer said, 'The shooter could easily have waited and turned his gun on other people in the Mumtaz but he hadn't. Why? Instead, he walked straight out. His escape seemed to have been well planned because he knew which alley to dart down as he fled.'

Donald Glue, his wife and two young daughters went on to suffer nightmares and post-traumatic stress from what they witnessed that day. Mr Glue went over the scene time and time again in his head. He said, 'I didn't think he was a bad guy at first. I thought it was someone the waiter knew. '

Marion Flaws said, 'There was some blood on the floor but not very much, which made it all feel even less real. The body of Shamsuddin Mahmood was lifeless by this time, though. We all knew he'd died.' She said that a lot of what happened seemed to occur in slow motion. It only snapped back into real time when she reached the landline phone in the back of the restaurant and dialled 999. 'They put me through to police headquarters in Inverness because I didn't have the direct phone number for the local Kirkwall police station.'

But Inverness was more than one hundred miles away and the Chinook helicopter crash had diverted all vital emergency services, leaving virtually no police on duty. It took at least another five minutes for officers to contact their colleagues in Kirkwall. Back inside the restaurant, customers looked on in stunned disbelief. As Marion Flaws later said, 'None of us could quite believe what had just happened but poor Shamol was lying dead on floor as evidence of the reality of the situation.'

First on the scene was a local doctor who just happened to be attending a function a few hundred yards away and had already heard about the incident. He immediately pronounced the victim dead but advised Marion and everyone else in the restaurant to stay on the premises until the police arrived. 'There was a killer out there somewhere,' Flaws said. 'It was difficult to be there with the body nearby but we all recognised that we were most probably safer inside than anywhere else.'

At the same public toilets on nearby Kiln Corner – where he'd prepared for his kill just a few minutes earlier – the man in the balaclava locked himself in a cubicle and frantically began ripping off his clothes and replacing them with new ones from a backpack he now had in his hands. At that moment, BT telephone engineer Johnny Rendall walked in to the toilets and heard banging and rustling coming from a cubicle. The man in the cubicle emerged just as Rendall was finishing using the urinal but he only got a glimpse of the back and left side of the man's head as he left the toilets and began striding purposefully up a road leading away from the town centre. Rendall said, 'I'll never forget the way that man was walking. He was stooping like a guy on a military training mission. I was in the army myself, so I knew he must have had services training at the very least. He was crouching low. It was as if he had a plan and he was executing it by exiting the town through a carefully thought-out route.'

Rendall also noticed the man was not just walking with his head down but had his hands tucked firmly into his pockets. He seemed to have a 'bit of an attitude' and appeared 'charged up'. Rendall estimated his height as between five foot ten and six foot one. The man was wearing a navy-blue, padded sweatshirt with a hood covering his head. He also wore blue jeans with a patch on them. So, just a few minutes after shooting dead an innocent restaurant manager, the killer was heading out of Kirkwall on his own two feet, seemingly without a care in the world, having completed his 'mission'. It was 7.30 p.m. and no doubt the shooter would have heard the police and ambulance sirens wailing in the distance as he made his escape out of town.

# 10.

BACK AT THE Mumtaz, those same police sirens were getting closer. Local police officers eventually arrived at the restaurant ten minutes after Marion's 999 call.

Michael Ross later claimed that at about 7.10 p.m. that evening he turned his bicycle round and headed back up the hill towards his home in St Ola. He said, 'I cycled back home by the same route I'd come. When I was outside the gates of Bignold Park, I heard the sound of sirens. I did not see the vehicle with sirens but it sounded like they were in the area of the pier. I just cycled straight home. I did not see anyone that I know on the way.'

Ross later backtracked and changed his story by saying he didn't leave Kirkwall town centre until about 8 p.m. But he continued to insist he was nowhere near the sea front area where the Mumtaz was located. Ross also later admitted he didn't actually reach home until 8.30 p.m., which was more than an hour after the shooting. Whatever the truth of the matter, at some stage Michael Ross started pumping his bike up that big hill back towards St Ola. Behind him in Kirkwall, a heinous, cold-blooded crime had just changed the lives of many people for ever.

At 7.40 p.m., Eddy Ross got a phone call from Kirkwall police station telling him about the shooting. He was at home with his young daughter so he drove her to his mother's home in the centre of Kirkwall and then headed to the restaurant. On arrival at the Mumtaz, Eddy was instructed by senior officers to interview witnesses inside the restaurant. According to his testimony to police, Michael eventually arrived back at the house and found no one in. He took the family's two lurcher dogs, Skye and Tor, for a walk in a nearby field. He could see down into the town of Kirkwall from where he was and must have watched avidly as ambulances and police cars buzzed around the distant streets, blue lights flashing and sirens wailing.

Michael's mother Moira returned to the house at about 8.30 p.m. Michael appeared back at the house with the dogs at about 8.40 p.m. and she told her oldest son that his policeman father had been called out because a murder had been committed in the town. Michael didn't bat an eyelid.

In Kirkwall town centre, new customers arriving at the Mumtaz were politely turned away by police officers, including Eddy Ross. None of the new customers even noticed Mahmood's corpse crumpled up on the carpeted floor. If they had, they would have seen a short trail of blood where he had clutched at his wound before collapsing to the ground. One of the first policeman at the scene later recalled, 'There was little blood and it was hard at first to grasp that this man had just been shot dead.'

One customer recalled, 'I couldn't take my eyes off him. Everyone was rushing around the restaurant but my eyes were on that poor man.'

The police ordered all customers who had been present during the shooting to stay inside the restaurant while officers including Eddy Ross spoke to them and made an initial search for any incriminating evidence that could link the killer to his crime. Mahmood's colleagues, including the waiter Khukon Uddin and owner of the restaurant Moina Miah, were in pieces. 'I saw them crying,' said Marion Flaws. 'He was their friend and colleague.'

A customer told police, 'It looked like a contract killing to me.'

Throughout, the body of Shamsuddin Mahmood remained on the floor of the restaurant. Some customers were eventually escorted around the corner to Kirkwall's police station to give statements. Flaws was allowed to go to her home nearby after agreeing to talk to officers later.

While bewildered local police tried to lock down the scene of the crime, detectives from police headquarters in Inverness were hurtling north on the slow and twisting A9 road up the east side of Scotland to Scrabster, to catch a ferry to the islands. The police departments' only helicopter had been seconded by emergency services investigating the Chinook helicopter crash.

At the Mumtaz, local police, including Eddy Ross, cordoned off the restaurant with yellow crime scene tape. Ross had a reputation among his colleagues as a bit of a prickly character but there was no doubting his devotion to his job. Eddy had dropped everything and jumped in his car the moment he heard on his police radio what had happened. He was well-known in the community as a keen marksman, a man who spent much of his leisure time either on the local gun range or out hunting rabbits, geese and deer in the barren hills behind Kirkwall. Ross was also renowned for collecting guns and ammunition in much the same way others collect racing pigeons. But Eddy always insisted he kept his armoury one hundred per cent secure. Eddy and two colleagues told their superiors they were happy to stand guard outside the Mumtaz restaurant all night if necessary. Word had spread fast in Kirkwall and most folk didn't want to leave their homes in case they came face to face with the killer on the loose. Not surprisingly, the town of Kirkwall went into a complete lockdown.

The special squad of murder detectives from the Highland and Islands division, in Inverness, finally arrived in Kirkwall in the early hours. The division was the most northerly force in the UK and covered a geographical area the size of Belgium but murders were relatively unusual. And this was the first murder in the Orkneys for twenty-five years.

The following morning should have been a busy shopping day for the locals but the streets of the centre of Kirkwall were completely deserted. Local and mainland police launched a massive manhunt. Every police officer on the islands plus reinforcements from the mainland had been ordered to join. Cordons were established at the airport and ferry terminals. A trained unit of armed police from the mainland were also on standby. As special operations were mounted at airfields and harbours, each car and every passenger was searched and questioned. Everyone leaving Orkney in the three days following the murder had to complete a form for follow up at a later date. Those persons were then traced. But there was no immediate suspect and no clear motive. Many of the islanders were in a panic, locking doors when there was never any need to in the past. One young girl kept her horse in the house because she was afraid it might be attacked. The local radio station replaced the usual slots on missing pets with murder inquiry updates.

Head of the team of detectives from the mainland was Detective Superintendent George Gough, the senior detective at the Highlands force, who was just as devastated as the islanders. He said, 'To think that someone would do this for no apparent reason . . . it could be someone who came into the islands or one of their own – we just don't know.'

Every person going in and out of Kirkwall would be stopped and identified at roadblocks on all the main roads out of town. Every house in the islands' capital was to be visited and each home across the Orkneys contacted. A murderer was on the loose and no one knew if he or she was going to strike again.

Initially, theories as to the motive behind the murder were few and far between. Officers wondered if it was drug or debt related, or maybe a crime of passion, perhaps involving a contract killing. And they only had two pieces of evidence – the 9mm bullet that had killed Shamsuddin Mahmood instantly and its casing. The bullet had lodged itself in the wall behind where he was shot.

They had no forensic or witness evidence linking anyone to the crime scene and no murder weapon. It was going to be an uphill struggle.

# 11.

AT 9 A.M. ON the morning after the murder, Eddy Ross – still on duty outside the Mumtaz restaurant – was asked by Inverness-based scene-of-the-crime officer Detective Constable Peter 'PJ' MacDonald to join him and a civilian assistant inside the premises to carry out some forensic examinations.

One former colleague said, 'Eddy was the islands' unofficial ballistic expert, so it made complete sense for him to help the officers examining the scene of the murder.'

Ross later recalled, 'PJ asked me to come in and asked me to look at the empty [bullet] case. I am not a firearms expert, I don't like that term, but I have a considerable knowledge of the subject.' Ross got down on his knees on the floor of the Mumtaz restaurant to look at the bullet-casing lying on the ground and then looked up at the bullet lodged in the wall. 'I did not touch it, but held a torch on the base of the case for the identification markings.' He later said, 'I think there were four different types of markings – three of the four I identified, but the fourth one I was not sure about.'

The priority at that early stage of the enquiry was to examine any potential evidence. Inside the restaurant, officers stood by as Ross then carefully re-examined the bullet and casing without touching them, so as not to forensically 'infect' the evidence. A fellow officer said later, 'That bullet was crucial. We all knew that it might be the best bit of evidence we would ever have to try and identify the shooter. Eddy also knew this and painstakingly examined it over and over again.'

Ross looked closely at the firing pin indentation on the bullet casing as well and noticed it had a very light indentation on the primers. He later said, 'This meant that there had been no adjustment made to the pistol in relation to its use with 2Z rounds, which are used in machine guns and therefore have harder primers.'

Examining the bullet still embedded in the plasterboard wall, Ross was able to deduce that it was standard rifling on the bullet with a right-hand twist. He then got another look at the bullet casing after it was bagged by investigators and later said that from markings on the rim it was obvious that it was not a 'virgin round' and would appear to have been chambered on previous occasions. Ross was later accused by some colleagues of walking into the crime scene uninvited but he insisted this was not the case. He said, 'The restaurant was a scene of crime and you do not enter any crime scene without invitation.'

Not one of his police colleagues raised an eyebrow at his detailed assessment because they all knew him to be an 'expert', albeit unofficial. Ross also told detectives the bullet must have been from a standard 9mm pistol. He later said, 'From the position where the casing lay in relation to where the bullet was embedded in the wall, I was able to deduce that the weapon was a semi-automatic pistol with a right-hand ejection in a forward direction.'

One of Eddy's colleagues later said, 'I remember Eddy looked at that bullet slowly and deliberately. He was proud of his expert knowledge and clearly enjoyed the fact that the other officers needed his input.'

Ross announced to his colleagues that he would check out the fourth set of unknown markings on the casing through reference books when he got home at lunchtime. He eventually arrived back at *Tjörn* at around 1 p.m. 'I spoke to my wife and told her what was going on,' he said later. In his study that lunchtime, Eddy Ross looked through gun reference books to check the markings for the particular type of bullet he'd just seen at the Mumtaz. Eventually, he was able to establish that the initials 'KF', found on the bullet, stood for the Kirkee Arsenal in India.

Ross's assessment to his colleagues back at the Mumtaz that afternoon so impressed both the local police and the mainland detectives that they instructed him to locate every 9mm gun on the islands and test them. They needed to know quickly if the murder weapon was still in circulation. Most who encountered Eddy Ross during that first twenty-four hours following the Mahmoodmurder didn't notice anything strange about the officer's response to the biggest true crime story the Orkneys had ever seen. One explained, 'Eddy was the consummate professional. He was diligent in everything he did as a police officer. We always reckoned it was down to his early days in the army.'

However, one colleague did say he was struck by Eddy Ross's 'detached' demeanour. The officer said, 'He seemed very emotionless about the shooting. I never heard him voice any sympathy for the victim and in some ways he acted as if nothing out of the ordinary had even happened.'

Just after Ross and his police colleagues examined the only pieces of concrete evidence left behind by the killer, young waiter Uddin, who'd shared the flat above the restaurant with Mahmood, told detectives he had the dead man's diary. He told police that they would find details of Mahmood's family in the diary. However, that diary was never picked up from the apartment above the Mumtaz because the police forgot all about it.

Meanwhile, the Orkneys' lockdown continued. Even flights to the city airport were suspended. A killer was on the loose in one of the most isolated communities in Britain. Residents grabbed whatever weapons they had to hand, including an arsenal of legal firearms. After all, more than sixty per cent of the islands' population of twenty thousand people owned guns.

The Orkneys' most senior police officer, Chief Inspector Alistair MacLeod, admitted to the media that the killer might have already slipped back on to the mainland. MacLeod feared the wanted man had used one of the many deserted inlets that existed along the islands' craggy coastline and were ideal places for a boat to pick someone up. MacLeod also admitted it was equally possible the killer had gone to ground on the islands and would lie low for some time before trying to leave. Unfortunately, this statement had the knock-on effect of making Orcadians even more fearful for their own personal safety.

Homicide detectives across the world have long recognised that the most crucial period of time after a murder is the twenty-four hours following the crime. 'If you haven't nabbed the killer by then, there is a good chance you'll never solve it,' one retired Scotland Yard detective said. But the police in Kirkwall couldn't even fathom if the murder had any back story. Where was the motivation? And even more importantly, where was the scientific evidence? There was nothing other than a bullet-casing and a bullet lodged in the wall behind where the victim had been standing when he was shot.

During that first twenty-four hours a number of strange incidents occurred that, on later reflection, may well have been deliberate 'red herrings' planted by someone connected to the killer in order to distract the ongoing police investigation. The first incident was the sighting of a man wearing a balaclava, driving a car in the town of Stromness, fifteen miles from Kirkwall. The same day, a number of discarded balaclavas were found scattered across the area. One was in the village of Deerness, twelve miles east of Kirkwall and another was in Stromness. Were others protecting the killer by sprinkling false clues around the islands like confetti? Had these 'incidents' been ordered by the killer or someone close to him?

Meanwhile, Kirkwall police contacted their colleagues in Southampton, where Shamsuddin Mahmood's brother Bulbul Shafiuddin and his family lived. Two officers discovered Mr Shafiuddin was on a trip to Bangladesh and his devastated wife, Ruby, was then asked to identify certain items belonging to her brother-in-law as part of the identification process. She collapsed and her husband later said that the murder had a serious effect on her mental health. She was also terrified that the killer might come to her home to get her and her daughters.

The Thursday deadlines of two local Kirkwall weekly newspapers meant they weren't able to publish the story of the murder until eight days later and the Scottish national papers had a field day when they splashed the story across their front pages on 4 June 1994. Everyone was completely flummoxed by the killing. It didn't make any sense and neither newspapers nor TV news really knew how to handle the story at first. Talk of a hit man seemed far-fetched but most of the media went with that angle initially because it was sensational and would no doubt help sell newspapers. But most of the reporters covering the early days of the police investigation later admitted they didn't believe it had been a hit man from the outset.

One veteran crime reporter later said, 'It was quite simply one of the most bizarre stories I've ever covered. The police didn't have a clue, either. I think the hit man angle was clutched out of the sky just to try and make it look as if the police had some kind of inside track, which of course they did not.' Initially, detectives had refused to name the victim in public. 'If they had then all this hit man stuff would have been laughed at and dismissed immediately,' said the reporter. Detectives later insisted it was normal policy not to name a murder victim until all his relatives had been contacted. 'But they shot themselves in the foot because it wasn't hard to get the victim identified. Everyone in Kirkwall knew who it was within hours of it happening.'

Restaurant owner Moina Miah had actually given the victim's name away without even realising the police had decided not to publicise it. He told reporters on the scene how Shamsuddin Mahmood had arrived seven weeks earlier from London and didn't have an enemy in the world. Not surprisingly, Miah reiterated to reporters that he and the rest of his staff would not feel safe until the killer was apprehended.

Miah, his family and eighteen-year-old waiter Khukon Uddin had been taken to a secret location in Kirkwall hours after the killing. Miah was as bewildered as the police about the motive behind the attack. 'He didn't have any enemies and we haven't got any enemies,' he told reporters. 'As far as I know no one has got a grudge against us. We are now really scared – we think that whoever did this could come after us as well. We feel we need protection until this man is caught.'

Meanwhile, some citizens were so terrified by the murder that they began contacting the police about any suspicious people in their midst. One group of visitors to the island staying in a bed-and-breakfast in the picturesque hamlet of St Margaret's Hope on the nearby island of South Ronaldsay were hauled out of their beds and taken to Kirkwall police station. All the alleged suspects were later released without charge but there were rumours they were 'not white' and that was the only reason they were targeted.

Some Orcadians – particularly those in Kirkwall – were already feeling a slight sense of shame about the murder, even though there was no apparent motive. The island's council convener, Hugh Halcro-Johnston, told one reporter: 'This is just not something that happens in Orkney. It's something we see on television and something we hear about happening in other areas.' This perfectly reflected the attitude of many Orcadians. They saw the murder as something unreal, comparable to what they watched on TV every night. And by voicing their sentiments, it gave many citizens some distance from the reality of the situation. It was as if they were saying, 'It didn't really happen. It's just something off the telly.'

The so-called 'crack team' of detectives drafted in from Inverness were still struggling with the most basic lines of enquiry. The victim himself had only been in Orkney for a relatively short time, so it was hard to establish any of his history. DS Gough then reiterated his belief that the killer was most likely a local person or certainly a person remaining in Orkney. His rationale was that the perpetrator appeared to know his bearings. After all, once the killer was seen running up the lane away from the restaurant, he was not seen again. This was a man who knew his way around Kirkwall. There were many places that a person could lie low on the Orkneys Islands and it didn't help that the Inverness detectives were unfamiliar with the area. Many in Kirkwall were deeply disturbed by the suggestion that the killer was a local. This implied the killer must have had a link to a victim who was a man from Bangladesh. How could that possibly be the case?

# 12.

WATCHING ALL THE police and media activity from the safety of his cliff top family home overlooking Scapa Flow was Michael Ross. It's impossible to know if he already feared arrest as a potential suspect or whether his father had assured him he would protect his son whatever had really happened. But more 'red herrings' appeared a few days after the murder.

An army cadet known to Michael Ross jumped out at the owner of the Mumtaz and his children near the restaurant. The cadet was wearing a cadet balaclava and he was with a friend who later gave a statement to police about the incident. But the motive behind this incident has never been fully explained. A number of Kirkwall residents informed the police that two days before the murder, two men were involved in a late-night argument with Shamsuddin Mahmood outside the Mumtaz restaurant. Attempts to find the others involved proved fruitless initially. However, it was said that the clash between the victim and some 'local youths' was peppered with racist remarks by the teenagers and one of the youths said, 'I'll shoot you,' as they left the scene.

With the cordon thrown around Orkney's air and sea terminals bringing no further breakthroughs in the investigation, enquiries were further extended to take in other Bangladeshi communities in the south of England, where Shamsuddin Mahmood had put down roots. Everyone in Kirkwall presumed the cold-blooded killing would be headline news across the nation over the following few days but the Chinook army helicopter crash dominated the newspapers and TV news bulletins. A rumour suddenly spread around Kirkwall suggesting the killer *was* a professional hit man after all and he'd flown off the island from Kirkwall's airport an hour after the shooting in a private plane. It was discovered that the plane had, in fact, been chartered by ITN news reporters and crew already on the islands to film another documentary when they were ordered to head to the Mull of Kintyre to cover the helicopter crash.

The early days of the police investigation smacked of desperation as far as many locals were concerned. It seemed as if the authorities had no idea who they were looking for and this panicked residents, already fearing that they could be the killer's next victim. A possible racist motive in the killing was played down by police, initially. Many locals engaged in wild speculation as one Kirkwall citizen explained: 'I clearly remember one neighbour telling me that he was convinced the victim had been killed because he was involved in some kind of drug-smuggling ring. The same man also made it clear that because the victim was black, Kirkwall's white residents had nothing to fear because the murder was "a bunch of blacks fighting over drugs turf" . . . I was stunned by what this man was saying but like most people in Kirkwall I didn't know how to respond. Maybe this man was right? But it didn't make sense and I hated myself for even thinking he might have been correct.'

Within days of the murder, the community had begun splitting itself into two distinct camps. A former Kirkwall resident said, 'I don't want anyone to know I am saying this, even today, all these years later, but the attitude of some in the Orkneys is just as troubling now as it was back then . . . the older, more traditional residents – most of whom were born and bred on the islands – were clearly implying that because the victim was black that meant it didn't really matter as much as if a white resident had been murdered. The other camp were less open about their feelings because some were weary of clashing with the old-time, traditional brigade. I personally wish we'd all been more vocal about our feelings back then because then these racist slurs might have been drowned out but that isn't the case, even today.'

Up in the small hamlet communities overlooking Kirkwall, the racist connotations swirling around the murder could be heard even louder. One local businessman later told reporters: 'Those Indians at the restaurant were up to no good. There were drugs involved and that's why that Indian fella got shot. It was nothing to do with us . . . it's obvious, isn't it? These people come here to the islands, invade our shores and then behave badly. Why is it so hard for people to accept that this man obviously had it coming to him?'

But were the local police feeling the same way as some of the residents? One former officer said, 'We were still treating this as an unexplained murder. All that early stuff about hit men and drugs rings was nonsense and we recognised that very quickly after the killing.' However, some officers did imply in private they were convinced Mahmood had been 'up to no good', as the officer put it, 'There were a few officers who also made it clear that they didn't have any time for black people, whom they considered troublemakers and unwelcome on the islands.'

As the days passed following the murder more and more locals began to talk openly about a possible racist issue connected to the killing. Could it really be that a Kirkwall resident was capable of murdering a man because of the colour of his skin? The issue of race on the Orkneys certainly wasn't something that was mentioned in the guide books. But being black on the Orkneys always attracted attention, particularly when those people tried to live on the islands. Many had come away from the Orkneys talking of disturbing experiences that at least seem to suggest the islands remained frozen in a time warp. Certainly the islands themselves were dotted with no-frills villages that virtually ran themselves as autonomous communities. The centre of each village was usually a church plus a school and maybe a café and/or a general store. That was it. After all, this was (and still is) a place where in nature storms could blow up out of nowhere. Thunderheads often rock chimney tops and threaten vast waves. And those massive gusts of wind also push the clouds along at a frighteningly fast pace, which means sometimes even the worst day of weather could be punctuated by occasional glimpses of sunlight peeping through gaps in the clouds. It was an environment perfectly suited to isolationism, which often fuelled overt racism.

At the scene of the murder, detectives from the mainland meticulously 'swept' the restaurant in a desperate hunt for further clues but there was nothing. One local reporter later recalled, 'There was an eerie atmosphere on the streets of Kirkwall in the days following the murder. The town centre remained deserted. The islands were on a lockdown and locals genuinely feared for their lives. But the strangest thing of all was that no one seemed to have any expectations that the killer would be quickly apprehended. A man in a mask had walked into a restaurant and killed a waiter in cold blood but few expected the killer to be caught. We all presumed he'd left the island immediately and would probably never be arrested. It was this sense of apathy that was most disturbing. It was as if everyone just accepted that the worst crime in Orkney history had just been committed and there was absolutely nothing anyone could do about it.'

At the Orkney Short Bore Rifle Association headquarters, where Eddy Ross was chairman, he and another firearms expert friend tested all the 9mm pistols legitimately held in Orkney and also provided the Inverness squad of detectives with their membership names. Their painstaking examination concluded that none of the guns examined was the weapon used in the murder. But they *didn't* test any weapons connected to Ross himself, which included his 9mm Steyr that he claimed had a major barrel defect and couldn't be fired. Then there was his 9mm rim-fire saloon pistol, which he insisted was owned by a friend, plus a deactivated 7.65mm Browning pistol that had been wrongly classified as 9mm. Ross claimed that now belonged to another marksman friend. He also told colleagues that he couldn't find any sign of the same type of ammunition used by the shooter anywhere on the island.

On Saturday, 4 June, three days after the murder, a local

youth visited Kirkwall police station and admitted the murder victim had been arguing with him and another man a couple of days before the killing. Police referred to the exchange as an altercation that occurred after the waiter opened the front door of the restaurant. But police didn't feel the incident was significant enough at that stage to contribute towards helping them solve the murder, despite earlier claims that one of men had threatened to shoot Mahmood. Instead, detectives issued fresh appeals for the 'man' seen in and near the public toilets close to the Mumtaz restaurant to come forward so he could be eliminated from their enquiries.

The following day, a bullet cartridge case was found in the back of a taxi in Kirkwall and handed in to police. Detectives refused to discuss whether it was of significance to the enquiry. Again, this was later dubbed a blatant red herring, deliberately planted to confuse investigators. Police also received a vague report from a couple of local residents of a man running down a lane near the Mumtaz both before and after the killing. They concluded that it was highly likely this must have been the killer but the description wasn't detailed enough to be considered helpful.

That same Sunday, detectives then had what seemed to be a lucky break, something they desperately needed in order to move the murder enquiry in the right direction. A local mother and her seventeen-year-old daughter walked into Kirkwall police station, just a few hundred yards from the Mumtaz restaurant, and told officers they'd seen the killer 'practising' in woods a few weeks before the shooting. They insisted that the man had been dressed in similar clothes to the killer and at one point he'd even been wearing a balaclava. The man, they said, had been 'stalking' from tree to tree in

Papdale Woods. But it was the detail in the description by both mother and daughter that most impressed detectives. They even mentioned a waist-length, navy-blue, cotton jogging top being worn by the man. They'd also noticed two drawstrings for the hood and how the man was also wearing a black balaclava with one hole cut at eye level when he took his hood down. The two witnesses also both told how they then saw the man take off his balaclava and put it in the front pouch of his jogging top. Then, they recalled, he took the hooded top and put it in a rucksack with two shoulder straps. Both women even recalled that the straps were camouflage-coloured material made from nylon.

The pair also said the man was wearing a very distinctive sweatshirt, mainly white with a crew neck. There was a pattern with two lines running down across the top, one line red and the other turquoise, and the sweatshirt had an elasticated waist and neck-band. He was also wearing closely fitting blue jeans with black heavyweight army style combat boots with laces. The two women insisted the man's boots had two-inch heels to make him look taller than he really was. He also had a watch on his left wrist with a large face and brown leather strap. They described the man as five foot and seven inches tall, of stocky muscular build and about twenty-two to twenty-three years old, with blond/light brown hair. The hair style was longer on top and shorter at the sides. He had a wide neck with a broad face, a small, neat-ish nose and they remembered large, piercing eyes. Well-tanned but definitely white skinned. Not of foreign appearance, either and both women said they would definitely recognise the man again.

Detectives knew it was imperative to get these two prime

witnesses to identify the man himself but the women had not seen him anywhere in the town since the incident. No one at this stage realised that the 'man in the woods' was none other than Michael Ross, son of one of the first officers to arrive at the Mumtaz restaurant after the murder.

# 13.

THE FIRST EDITION of local weekly newspaper the *Orcadian* following the murder carried seven pages about the killing at the Mumtaz, including an appeal from Inverness detectives leading the murder hunt.

The *Orcadian* headlines that day summed up the confused state of the enquiry and the community. The paper's front page featured a story about a telephone threat made just before the murder against a woman whose phone number was listed in the local phone directory next to the Mumtaz restaurant. 'That story seemed a bit desperate,' said one local. 'How could you connect a call made to someone who just happened to have a number listed next to the Mumtaz with the murder? It was ridiculous.' But detectives assured journalists they thought the caller to the woman might well have been the same man who murdered Shamsuddin Mahmood. Police also disclosed in *The Orcadian* that the killer must have changed appearance in a nearby alleyway following the killing. As one

Kirkwall resident later said, 'That was hardly a masterstroke of police ingenuity. It was obvious the killer would have changed clothes.'

Another Kirkwall resident put it this way, 'It felt as if the police were trying to prove how hard they were working and how no stone was being left unturned. But it was having the opposite effect because many of us soon began to have absolutely no faith in the police.' At Kirkwall police station, local officers had been told to step back and leave the enquiry to the detectives from 'down south' as Inverness was referred to. A map of the area around the murder scene at the Mumtaz restaurant was also published in the local press. The Kirkwall resident said, 'But that didn't tell us anything we didn't already know. The whole investigation seemed to be stalling before it had even got going.'

Approximately one week after the murder at the Mumtaz, Michael Ross boasted to one of his classmates that he had a balaclava with three holes, just like the one that had been used by the murderer. Later he even admitted it was the one he wore in the woods during that 'ambush exercise' two weeks before the murder. Ross later claimed he took the balaclava to school after being pressurised to do so by his classmate. He said, 'My friend asked me to take it to school to show him. The next day I took it in but the boy was off sick. I just left it in my school bag.' Ross never actually showed the balaclava to anyone. After returning home in the evening, Ross's mother Moira found the balaclava in her son's bag. This sparked a furious row between Eddy and his son. Michael later admitted he was so shaken by the row that the following day he threw the balaclava in Scapa Flow. He said, 'I put a stone inside the balaclava and threw it off the cliff.' Two or three days later he threw another balaclava off the cliffs. This was a brown, open-faced one that he claimed he had found in a supermarket car park earlier in the year. Ross's mother put his hooded top in a jumble sale in nearby Finstown, to be sold for charity.

It was still early days as far as the murder investigation was concerned but detectives were mightily relieved to have stumbled on the evidence from that mother and daughter about the man in the woods. Officers were convinced it was the same man as the shooter. 'It felt right to us,' one Inverness detective later said. 'It all seemed to make sense.' Then a number of other witnesses came forward to talk about the incident and their accounts varied in relation to the height and build of the killer. On 9 June, police spoke to an eleven-year-old boy who'd seen the person in Papdale Woods. He had been walking home from school that afternoon and said the man was crouched down behind a wall beside a big tree and was wearing a black top with a hood and black mask on his face. The boy went home and told his mother. On 15 June, a seventeen-year-old schoolgirl – who'd been with the earlier young witness after she in turn had watched Michael Ross with her mother – informed police the man's posture was 'extremely odd'.

On the same day a fourteen-year-old boy was interviewed but his evidence was more vague than that of previous witnesses. The following day an even younger child came forward. By 19 June, the police had a total of seven witness statements regarding the incident in the woods. But detectives needed to move onto other aspects of the enquiry. They required more to nail the killer. And that's when the trail once again went stone cold.

Michael Ross attended army cadets on the last Wednesday

of June, three weeks after the murder. He got talking to a teenage girl he'd dated the previous year and told her how he sometimes carried his father's guns around with him. That girl later recalled, 'He knew that I was worried about the gun used in the murder and he told me that I should tell the police about it if I wanted to.' The girl was stunned by what Ross said to her. But at the same time she was impressed that he was being so open about it and encouraging her to go to the police if she felt it was relevant.

Back in Kirkwall, Moina Miah and his family were no longer considered in danger and he reopened the Mumtaz a couple of weeks after the murder. As waitress Marion Flaws explained many years later, 'The carpet was cleaned and I carried on working there. Maybe there was a bit of new paintwork and a new patch of carpet but it wasn't re-decorated.' Initially, Mr Miah had planned to sell the premises and put adverts in a trade magazine and a Bengali newspaper but he admitted to locals that he didn't expect offers for it would be flooding in immediately. In fact, Miah didn't really want to sell the restaurant and move away from the Orkneys at all. He still hoped life would return to normal and initially many locals showed the restaurant support by going there.

Miah was determined not to be 'scared away'. He told one local newspaper reporter, 'I did not come here and spend money on the restaurant to move away again. Many customers have said, "Don't go, we need an Indian in Orkney." They have been very good to us. My staff can have a normal life now and my children are OK, too.' Miah said not only had there been no trouble in the restaurant since the killing but he was planning to recruit more staff to deal with an upturn in business.

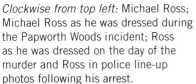

*Clockwise from top left:* Michael Ross; Michael Ross as he was dressed during the Papworth Woods incident; Ross as he was dressed on the day of the murder and Ross in police line-up photos following his arrest.

This is a true letter. I promise that I saw the person who killed the Indian waiter. I saw his face in full and the hand-gun. It was in toilets at Kiln corner. I have lived long enough with the guilt of not coming forward.

The person was about 15+ years approx - white, and had a balaclava on head but still not turned down, colour was either dark blue or black dark clothing. He came out of cubicle but went back in quick when he saw me. I looked over and saw his face in full. The hand gun was natural polished metal or silver and was like a big beretta.

This may sound stupid but the way he held hand-gun looked like he had handled a firearm before.

I just don't ken what to do!

Worried sick witness!

*Above:* The beach near the Ross home on which Michael Ross spent much of his early childhood.

*Below left*: The hand-written note by crucial witness Willy Grant that helped finally to bring the killer to justice.

*Below right*: The killer's protective father PC Eddy Ross on duty.

# Orcadian

Kirkwall, Thursday, June 9, 1994

43p

**SOLD**

THE MARK OF A QUALITY SERVICE

Est. 1854

SERVING CLIENTS – THE PEOPLE WHO MATTER

## 'This is it – your life's at an end'

### Mystery phone threat minutes before shooting

A chilling mystery phone call – threatening "This is it – your life's at an end" – was made shortly before Kirkwall restaurant manager Shamsudden Mahmood was gunned to death last Thursday evening, police have been told.

Yesterday detectives in the murder hunt declined to elaborate but it is understood that the phone call was received by an Orkney woman whose telephone number is listed in the directory near that of the Mumutaz restaurant.

The woman immediately reported the call to Kirkwall police.

The man in charge of the murder investigation, which now extends the length of Britain from Orkney to Southampton, Detective Superintendent George Gough, would not comment on the significance, if any, of the call which at the time

had been dismissed as the work of a "crank".

Nor would he add to the news that a cartridge case, found on Sunday evening in the back of a Kirkwall taxi, had been handed into the local police station.

Police are now working on the possibility that the man responsible for last week's killing may have changed his apparent appearance as he ran down the lane next to the Mumutaz restaurant.

Detective Superintendent Gough said: "On Bridge Street he is described by a couple of witnesses as wearing a dark coloured jacket, but, at the other end

of the lane a man comes out about that time, described as wearing a mustard coloured or khaki top with its hood up.

"My favoured option at the moment is that these were the same man.

There is also the description of a man running in the lane who is a white man. Whether or not it's the man who came in at the top or the man who came out at the bottom is debatable – we cannot say. We need to trace that man as well or anyone who saw such a person wearing a top with a hood up and which they considered to be khaki or mustard."

Detective Superintendent

Gough declined to say whether the jacket may have been a reversible one or not.

"The man coming out of the bottom of the lane was running as well," he added.

Mr Gough also wants to hear from two men heard arguing with Mr Mahmood only two days before the shooting. "About midnight on the night of May 31, that is Tuesday night, there was an altercation at the door of the restaurant when the now deceased answered the door. There were two men arguing with him, trying to get into the restaurant.

"We do not know who these men are but they are white

as opposed to Asian. W would like these men to co forward and explain th matter to us.

"Tied to that, there wa three other people in t restaurant at that ti believed to be local peo and if they can recall incident and come forwar help us we would appre that."

There is no obvious m for the killing at the mo although we are condu extensive backgrc checks.

Police are still interes tracing a man seen nea toilets that evening, we green trousers and to carrying a green rucksa

"Even if he has n whatsoever to do wi crime, it would help clarify the situatio eliminate him fro enquiries."

A police presence a of departure was still l yesterday but, because passage of time, che not now being carrie people there.

"My fear about th don't know whether the of the island, wh is local or anything conducted stop che filled in question people three days the murder and th hundreds."

Armed police available if req added.

House-to-hous are meantim extended. "At the is our intention here as long as i to try to establi of this murder all main lines of

"Only by goin and speaking to they appre significance o saw."

Description and three witn being issued t the public, officers visiti and hotels. Police have moment to photofit pict enact the crin are not ex extended abro all lines are t in this coun forces in Southampt helping.

*The victim of last Thursday evening's shooting at the Mumutaz Indian Restaurant, 26-year-old Shamsudden Mahmood.*

## Police dragnet for gunman as murder horror shocks Orkney

The violent face of Britain shattered the calm of Orkney last week when, in a single act of horror, a man was gunned down in full view of a room full of diners, including families with children, at the local Indian restaurant.

Orkney's first murder since 1969 left shock and alarm as police were called to the popular restaurant early on Thursday evening when restaurant manager Mr Shamsudden Mahmood (26) was shot and fatally wounded by an unknown assailant.

Around a dozen shocked diners, including one family with children, looked on in horror as the masked and hooded man entered the restaurant in Kirkwall's Bridge Street and walked up to Mr Mahmood, who was sitting on tables at the time, shooting him in the face. The gunman then ran out, making his escape down a nearby

they ran down to the end of the street to get a doctor from nearby.

"There was obviously nothing anyone could have done for him though – he must have been shot at point blank range. One of the customers covered his face with a jacket. We all had to wait inside until the police were done. No-one has any idea of a motive for this crime," she added.

Mr Donald Glue of Willowburn Road, Kirkwall, who along family members were being served by Mr Mahmood at the time, declined to speak about the incident

Around the same time that evening another witness, who did not want to be named: "I could not say if it was before or after the killing and I only merely caught sight of him. He seemed to make off towards the harbour but he hesitated as if he was waiting for something and he could have gone in any direction

**TO PAGE FIVE**

A witness told The Orcadian that at first she had thought the hooded man had been sort of a joke but when Marian Flaws saw the gun he was about to be robbed. "I only feet away and back turned at the I was near the door ed it and turned to heard the shot but it happening.

He came out and other way and ran the lane there. I him as he ran Back Road but I see his top half the dyke there."

not say whether he Asian or white."

went back into

Police immediately sealed off the area around the Mumutaz and posted an all-night guard at the premises. (Picture: Orkney Photographic)

**CLOSED**

New Album: PURPLE

Video Rental:
ADDAMS FAMILY 2, MY LIF

**north**

**McAdie & Re**

*Just About Anyth
Removals*

Removals – Storage
Fine Art – Pianos

*Above*: The Mumtaz restaurant in Kirkwall, Orkney, where waiter Shamsuddin Mahmood (inset) was murdered in 1994.

*Below*: The Royal British Legion branch in Kirkwall where Eddy Ross often held court. *Inset*: Eddy Ross, Michael Ross at a Black Watch event.

Meanwhile, detectives travelled to the south of England to speak to people who'd worked with the victim when he lived with his brother Bulbul Shafiuddin in the Southampton area. They discovered Mahmood came from a prosperous Bangladeshi family. He was a perfectly law-abiding and respectable citizen. The family of the dead man told detectives they suspected that their brother had been killed because of the colour of his skin. They also revealed that Shamsuddin Mahmood had a girlfriend back in Bangladesh but she was so young that the relationship wasn't socially acceptable, which was one of the reasons that Mahmood had travelled to the UK. Police enquiries also revealed that the victim's work visa had run out the previous May. Some in Kirkwall would later suggest that this meant Shamsuddin Mahmood was a dangerous criminal and that it explained why he was murdered.

It was certainly possible that Mahmood's main reason for being in the Orkneys may have been because he thought it might take authorities longer to find him once his visa had run out. But that didn't make him a cold-blooded criminal on the run.

Bulbul Shafiuddin also admitted to police there had been a dispute between himself and his dead brother about a family inheritance. But, again, that was hardly a motive for hiring a hit man – or was it?

Officers quickly announced that nothing in Mahmood's background suggested a real motive for his murder. The few Orkney people Mahmood came into social contract with described him as a happy-go-lucky character. Amanda Rosie, a taxi driver, told detectives of their relationship, 'He was never a boyfriend, just a good friend. Like most young lads he liked going out for a drink. He was such a good-natured person and full of fun. He was never a guy who would hurt anyone and he never spoke of any trouble.'

After completing their enquiries in the south of England, high-ranking Inverness officer Gordon Urquhart made a point of publicly stating that the victim was innocent of any nefarious activities that could have led to his murder. But some locals in Kirkwall remained convinced that Shamsuddin Mahmood was the kingpin behind some kind of global drugs empire that had resulted in a hit man sneaking on to the Orkneys and murdering him in cold blood. Many of the same 'negative' individuals, who'd coldly dismissed the murder as a gangster contract killing, then also claimed Shamsuddin Mahmood was involved in protection rackets on the Scottish mainland. Again, no evidence was ever found to back up these claims.

However, detectives had already made one glaring error following the murder. They'd 'forgotten' all about the diary that had been offered to them shortly after the killing. In all likelihood, the diary may have contained further clues as to Shamsuddin Mahmood's character and lifestyle that might have helped investigators. Meanwhile, second-in-command of the mainland detectives, Detective Inspector Angus Chisholm, continued his search of the islands for anyone who owned the Kirkee 9mm bullets used in the murder. These were the bullets Eddy Ross had first told him about. Over one hundred statements were taken from gun club members, from other persons registered to keep firearms and anyone with an interest in shooting.

As is often the case in investigations, the need for clues to stoke the fires of the media coverage were essential but they were going out very rapidly. As one mainland journalist later said, 'We all needed more information so that we could keep pushing the story along in journalistic terms but there was this huge void appearing with no new developments and it had the effect of pushing the story off the front pages very rapidly.' This was bad news for detectives desperate to publicise the shooting as much as possible in the hope it might jog someone's memory that would then provide them with a breakthrough clue. The police also had to contend with yet another rumour about the victim. This time it was being said that he was some kind of spy and he'd been eliminated by his nation's enemies.

One former policeman on the island later said, 'I'm not even sure that Bangladesh has a spy service. It was a ludicrous rumour but it summed up the state of the investigation in those early days and weeks.'

At the end of June 1994, an article in the *Orcadian* revealed that lead detective DS Gough had been recalled to his Inverness headquarters 'for the time being' due to the pressure of other ongoing investigations. Many in Kirkwall were upset by the way the mainland police began to return to Inverness so soon after the murder and there were rumblings in the town that the police seemed to be taking the investigation 'too lightly'. Taking over the day-to-day enquiries would be his deputy, DI Chisholm, who immediately issued a fresh appeal for witnesses. DI Chisholm also asked PC Eddy Ross to come up with an address for the Kirkee Arsenal. He needed to find out how the bullet had been distributed.

In early July 1994, Ross bumped into former marine and old school friend Jim Spence, now working as a road sweeper on the streets of Kirkwall town centre. Spence was a shy, quiet type of character and he'd always found himself a little in awe of people like Ross, especially down at the British Legion clubhouse in Kirkwall. Spence had read in the *Orcadian* the news that police knew the bullet that killed Shamsuddin Mahmood came from an Indian arsenal. That meant the bullet could have come from the sealed or opened boxes of 9mm Indian bullets that he'd given to Ross back in 1984. The local newspaper had quoted a police firearms expert, saying, 'Asian origin is not necessarily significant as such Indian-made ammunition is commercially available in this country. Military surplus ammunition like this is widely advertised in gun magazines and any registered firearms dealer can get it although, in this particular case, one would assume it was bought on the black market. There is so much stuff coming into Britain from Eastern Europe these days.'

During that first meeting following the murder, Ross and Spence discussed Spence's bullets. He later recalled, 'I think he asked me if I had any more or knew where I could get any more because he'd used up the bullets at a local shooting range.' Spence tried to nervously laugh it off by saying there were thousands of those same bullets in circulation if Ross wanted any more. 'I told him that I didn't have any more and I had given all of them to him.' Spence was no doubt starting to deeply regret ever getting involved with Eddy Ross in the first place. He kept thinking about that car park all those years earlier, when they met and he handed over all those bullets to Ross. He'd always thought that Ross wanted the bullets for his gun club and that he would have fired them all off in practice within a few months of getting them. But now Spence was starting to wonder if one of those bullets had been used to kill a man.

# 14.

THERE WAS ONE consistent characteristic of the killer suggested by many witnesses and it was finally the subject of much debate at Kirkwall police station's hastily established murder inquiry room.

Was the shooter in the military?

If so, there were literally thousands of current and ex-servicemen living on the islands. It would be like looking for a needle in a haystack. And as one recently retired local policeman later said, 'If they'd decided to find a soldier more quickly, then they might have had a faster breakthrough on the job.'

It was getting towards the end of July 1994 and police had already interviewed thousands of people. They'd even enlisted the help of Interpol, who tracked down dozens of foreign tourists visiting the islands at the time of the murder. At the top of that steep hill to St Ola, Michael Ross was feeling quietly confident about his predicament. He knew there were people in Kirkwall who might make wild accusations against him but he still felt on a 'high' in some ways. When he bumped into the ex-girlfriend whom he'd been planning to avenge with that attack on that boy in Papdale Woods, Michael Ross got a further boost to his ego. After he'd told the girl about his intended revenge attack on the boy who hit her, she encouraged him to give the other boy 'a good hiding'. This type of reaction to violence was music to the ears of someone like Michael Ross. Yet, whatever racist remarks later attributed to Michael Ross, his father still saw nothing wrong with his own interest in Adolf Hitler and the Nazi Party.

Meanwhile, as he cleaned the streets of Kirkwall, Jim Spence must have felt as though Eddy Ross was watching his every move during many weeks following the murder. Towards the end of the month, Ross made a second approach to Spence during which he made Spence 'extremely worried' about being implicated in the murder. Spence knew full well he'd given Ross one sealed and one opened box of the same 9mm Kirkee bullets as used by the shooter. Spence later insisted that at this second meeting Ross completely changed his story and told him that he'd thought about throwing the remaining bullets from that opened box into a local quarry but hadn't. This confused Spence because he thought Ross had said at their earlier meeting that he'd used all the bullets up on a firing range. Then Ross 'suggested' to Jim Spence that if asked by the police, he should say there was only ever one sealed box of 9mm Kirkee bullets. 'That's when he said he still had one box of them,' Spence later recalled.

Spence started to fear that Eddy Ross might have already named him as the supplier and that the police would soon want to speak to him, even though it had been many years since Spence gave the bullets to Ross. He pointed out to Ross that he'd also given him a box of .22 ammunition in addition to the two boxes of 9mm bullets. Spence asked if he should mention that to the police? According to Spence, Ross nodded and said, 'OK.'

At 6.20 a.m. on the morning of 11 August, Spence was sweeping the roads around Kirkwall town centre when he felt the presence of someone standing just behind him. It was PC Eddy Ross yet again. Spence's heart must have jumped a beat before he said a reluctant,' Hello, Eddy,' to that local bobby out on his beat. Spence told Ross that, if the police did approach him, he'd tell them he'd given him two boxes of bullets – the unopened one from the Kirkee Arsenal and a box of .22-calibre bullets that were not relevant to the murder case. But this time Ross clearly implied that he'd already handed some of the bullets into the police. He ordered the road sweeper only to only admit having given him one sealed box of those 9mm bullets, the same as the make used in the murder.

Ross murmured quietly, 'Remember, Jim. Just the one box.' When Spence didn't acknowledge what his friend had said, Ross repeated it again. 'Remember, Jim. Just the one box.' Spence was shaken and confused by Eddy Ross's attitude but tried to remain calm and nodded at Ross as he repeated his orders over and over again. Ross revealed that he was seeing a detective at 2 p.m. that day and they would want to see Spence immediately afterwards. As Spence tried to absorb the enormity of the situation, Eddy Ross calmly walked off in the opposite direction without even saying 'Goodbye'.

At 2 p.m., Ross went to Kirkwall police station and asked to speak to the murder squad's DI Chisholm. Ross told the officer that earlier that day he'd been checking through his ammunition box and 'found' the bullets by chance. Ross said, 'I intended to uplift some ammunition when I went south in the near future. I found a sealed box of thirty-five 9mm MK2Z, KF ammunition produced on 6 March 1972. The additional markings were not used on the rounds after 1965 and H3289 which may be a batch number, and D/I in a purple diamond mark which I don't know the significance of.'

Ross had just informed DI Chisholm that he possessed a sealed box of bullets the same in calibre and bearing similar numbers to those used by the killer in the murder of Mahmood. Then he handed the sealed box to the detective. Chisholm was stunned. Why hadn't Ross come forward with the bullets sooner? He recalled, 'It astonished me because we had been looking for these for several weeks before. That was the main focus of our inquiry.'

Ross then claimed that he either got the bullets from a local man or he might have picked them up while at the army shooting range in Bisley when he was in the Black Watch regiment. Ross insisted he needed to speak to the local man to confirm his involvement before putting his name forward to the enquiry. He didn't mention that he'd already seen Jim Spence at least three times in recent weeks. Ross said afterwards, 'I delivered the box to Angus Chisholm. I don't have and never have had any more of that ammunition, as far as I am aware. I wouldn't use this ammunition in my own guns because of the quality.'

Ross pointed out that the bullets were part of a massive consignment purchased by the British army, so his wasn't such a crucial admission. He insisted he just wanted to clear the air in case the finger of suspicion pointed at him. *PC Eddy Ross was the very same police officer whom detectives had earlier trusted to test all possible murder weapons on the islands in the aftermath to the murder.*

Ross phoned Spence a few minutes after leaving the police station and instructed Spence to report for interview at 6.30 p.m. On arrival, Jim Spence was shown the sealed box of 9mm bullets earlier handed to detectives by Ross. Spence told detectives he'd given Ross that same full, sealed box of Kirkee 9mm rounds and one box of .22 rounds (two boxes in total), despite Ross having ordered him to only admit to the one box. Detectives repeatedly asked Spence that night if he'd given Ross any more boxes of the Kirkee 9mm bullets and Spence insisted he had not. Immediately after Jim Spence left the police station, he was once again approached by Ross. Spence said that detectives had interviewed him for an hour and that they'd shown Spence just one box of ammunition and he'd informed detectives there was only ever one box.

'That's fine, Jim,' Ross told his old school friend. He didn't know that Spence had also mentioned the box of .22 bullets.

Ross later brushed off claims that he'd got Jim Spence to lie for him by saying, 'He was put under pressure by the police. Had I ever asked anyone to lie for me, which I never had done, I don't think Jim would have been the first one on my list.'

On the morning following his interview, Jim Spence was walking down to the municipal offices of Kirkwall town council to start work sweeping the streets when he passed the police station and noticed Eddy Ross cleaning a squad car on the station forecourt. Spence immediately ducked behind a wall to make sure Eddy Ross didn't see him.

Back up the hill, in windswept St Ola, the atmosphere inside the Ross family home must have been worsening. No doubt Eddy was now being doubly careful to always keep tabs on the key to his gun cupboard, which he usually kept on that piece of string tied around his neck. Ross pointed out at the time to all his close family and friends that if he'd had something to hide, surely he would have thrown all those bullets into the sea? As he later stated, 'That particular batch of munitions was in a box I kept full of odds and ends. But I knew I wouldn't be using it. It wasn't good quality.' Ross has always maintained that there were at least forty million rounds of that ammunition manufactured and that most of it had eventually been dumped because it was of such bad quality.

A couple of days later, on 14 August, Eddy Ross was contacted by detectives who wanted to 're-clarify the situation' re the bullets. They also wanted to know why Ross hadn't mentioned the box of .22 bullets that Spence described during his interview. Ross admitted that he'd actually received *three* boxes containing rounds of bullets from Spence, but insisted they consisted of one box of 9mm and two boxes of .22 rounds (one half-full). The detectives were bemused. Something wasn't right. Why would he lie in the first place about bullets that weren't relevant to the case? Detectives had already assumed that Ross coached Spence to lie about the other box of bullets. But now that lie had blown up in Ross's face. Ross had lost control of a dangerous situation through a combination of his own stupidity and Spence's nervousness. Friends of Ross later insisted that he and Spence had a 'misunderstanding' about the bullets. But detectives involved in the murder investigation suspected

Ross was trying to cover his tracks and maybe there was indeed another box of 9mm bullets that he was not telling them about.

But for the moment, they kept their distance from Ross and Spence. 'It seemed better to let them stew in their own juices for bit,' said one former Kirkwall officer. Instead, detectives decided to re-interview all the main witnesses in the hope they might remember something more that could then be used to put pressure on the pair.

On 16 August, a witness was re-interviewed who said he'd seen a balaclava-clad man crossing Junction Road towards the lane leading up to the Mumtaz Restaurant a few minutes before Mahmood's murder. This witness altered his story to say the man was slightly smaller, at between five foot and eight inches and five foot and ten inches and with a slim build. Two days later, investigators re-interviewed the ten-year-old child who'd seen the man in Papdale Woods. It had been more than two and half months since the murder but the boy provided more detail than he had in his previous testimony. This time he said that the person in the woods had also been in possession of a 'wooden object'. None of the other witnesses had mentioned such an item but to detectives this seemed a breakthrough because they believed that inside the wooden box could have been a weapon – maybe a gun and perhaps ammunition.

Meanwhile, 'bullet man' Jim Spence was having a lot of sleepless nights. Detectives knew he'd lied to them on behalf of Ross and every now and again they let Spence know through mutual acquaintances that he could well end up going to jail for covering up. Spence must have felt under immense pressure. But for the moment Ross was winning this particular war of nerves. He seemed to pose a bigger threat than murder squad detectives from Inverness.

On 21 August, police re-interviewed yet another Papdale Woods witness, who added very little to his previous account from 9 June, except commenting on the height of the person in the woods as being between five foot and six inches, and six feet. However, this witness was unable to put an age on the man in the mask.

'It appeared to many of us that the police were desperate,' said one Kirkwall resident. 'We'd all concluded that the killer was most likely long gone, so the danger to citizens was now minimal but the fact remained that out there somewhere was a cold-blooded killer.'

The re-interviewing of the Papdale Woods witnesses was seen by journalists and locals as yet more proof that the police investigation had stalled and they were clutching at straws. But, in fact, the opposite was true; detectives wanted to let the pressure continue to build on alleged co-conspirators Ross and Spence.

By this time, the police had spoken to twenty-one witnesses who'd seen the killer, fourteen inside the restaurant and an additional seven sightings of a man police believed to be the killer, either before he entered or after he exited the restaurant. A further two witnesses saw a man running from the end of the lane that the killer had used directly after the shooting wearing similar clothing but without his face masked. Nine witnesses of the twenty-one stated that the killer had a 'noticeable stoop', which was referred to in TV and newspaper reports. It was only when a PhotoFit picture was being prepared by detectives that an officer mentioned how much it resembled PC Ross's son Michael. Detectives knew they had to tread carefully. There was no actual proof so far to pin the murder on Michael Ross, although his father's connection to the bullet used in the killing did start to make detectives wonder if the man they were seeking had been on their doorstep all along.

In the middle of all this, the 'racist attitude' of some Orcadians seemed to be gaining momentum. As one Kirkwall resident explained, 'The longer the police failed to make an arrest, the more some people were basically saying, "It's just a black man who died. We need to move on with all this" . . . I remember thinking that the killer must have been laughing at all this. It felt like Kirkwall had decided to ignore the heartbreak and loss of life and move on. People were no longer studying their neighbours and friends as potential killers. No one seemed to want to think about what had happened just a few short months earlier.'

But the alleged involvement of Michael and Eddy Ross was now at the forefront of most detectives' minds. They were seriously contemplating for the first time that Shamsuddin Mahmood could have been murdered by a father and son 'assault team'.

As detectives quietly tried to gather in more evidence they then stumbled upon a number of disturbing stories about the suspect Michael Ross. There was talk among his classmates that Michael was a racist and that he'd been acting erratically in the months leading up to the murder. But again, this wasn't enough to pin a murder rap on Michael Ross. So detectives continued playing a waiting game.

# 15.

MONDAY, 28 AUGUST 1994 was Michael Ross's sixteenth birthday. It must have been a muted celebration considering that both Michael and his father Eddy were well aware that the detectives now had both of them in their sights.

At police headquarters in Kirkwall, mainland investigators led by Detective Inspector Chisholm continued to be patient as they worked around the clock on the case. They didn't want to make a move until they had enough to be certain they could nail Michael and Eddy Ross.

On 8 September, the mother and daughter witnesses from the Papdale Woods incident were out having coffee in Kirkwall town centre when they both saw 'the man from the woods' through the window eating a roll he'd bought in the shop opposite. The pair headed straight to a nearby phone box and tried to call the local police station but there was no answer. It wasn't until they got home fifteen minutes later that they finally reached the police. They told officers that the man was wearing the same distinctive white designer top underneath a blue top that he'd removed that day in the woods. One of the witnesses even did a drawing of the design for police. Police checked the CCTV from the town centre and found footage of the suspect but no one could positively identify him.

The following day, police officers accompanied the mother and daughter witnesses back to Albert Street in Kirkwall town centre where, by an amazing stroke of good fortune, they once again spotted and identified the same person from the previous day and the Papdale Woods incident. One of the attending police officers that day was able to name the man as Michael Ross because he knew Michael through his colleague, Eddy Ross. The two witnesses were taken to Kirkwall police station to complete a statement. The police were delighted. This could be the breakthrough they'd all been hoping for. Now they could surely step up the pressure on Eddy and Michael Ross. But the Inverness detectives knew they had to tread carefully because Eddy Ross was a wily character who would battle hard to ensure he and his son wriggled out of any charges unless they were airtight. So for the moment the police kept their cards close to their chests.

Back in windswept St Ola, that cloud hanging over the Ross household must have darkened considerably when Eddy heard from one of his colleagues at Kirkwall police station that his Michael had now been strongly linked to the murder. Ross later admitted that around this time he turned to his wife Moira and said, 'If he has done it, they will get it out of him.' And later that same day, Eddy asked his son, 'Did you shoot that man dead?'

'No,' replied Michael Ross as calmly as he could.

On 23 September, a TV crew arrived in Kirkwall to start

preparing an appeal for BBC's *Crimewatch UK* reconstruction programme. The police had decided not to reveal the alleged involvement of Michael and Eddy Ross in the hopes that a fresh appeal might provide them with more independent witnesses. But the following day, senior investigating officers approached Ross at the police station where he was working a shift on the front desk. Eddy was asked if Michael owned a sweatshirt similar to that in the sketch drawn by the main Papdale Woods witness. Eddy Ross confirmed he did. Eddy was then asked to bring Michael into the police station for questioning that afternoon. Officers assured Ross that if this initial interview was conducted voluntarily, then Michael could officially be classified as a 'witness', which meant no legal representation was necessary.

DI Chisholm and a colleague questioned Michael in the presence of his father and Michael insisted he was not the person in Papdale Woods that day in May. Michael also provided an alibi for his movements on the night of the murder by insisting he met two friends when he was cycling around the Eastbist estate. The teenage schoolboy was remarkably calm during the interview. Chisholm later said, 'Although he was only sixteen he appeared very mature for his age. He was calm, reflective in his answers. Nothing at all fazed him.' Chisholm did not reveal that Michael had been identified by those two Papdale Woods witnesses in person in the town centre a couple of weeks earlier.

The decision to allow Eddy Ross to sit in on the interview with his son was later heavily criticised. After all, he had previously handed in bullets of the same type used in the murder, so it was highly irregular to allow him to be present during this interview of his son in relation to the same crime.

And Michael was by this point over sixteen and could have been legally interviewed on his own. The Ross family and friends later claimed that the presence of Michael's father during the interview had prevented Michael from admitting to his conduct in Papdale Woods because he didn't want to 'disappoint' his father.

While at Kirkwall police station, Michael also agreed to have his photo taken. One shot showed him in a white sweatshirt that looked like the one described by the Papdale Woods witnesses. But not even posing in front of a camera seemed to bother the teenager. As one former officer later said, 'He was so chilled out. I felt at the time he must have been coached by his father to remain impassive throughout the interview.' It was frustrating for the detectives who'd believed that once they had Michael under their interrogation spotlight, he'd soon crack. But the Ross family were clearly made of much sterner stuff than most. No doubt Eddy had drilled it into his two sons to trust no one, not even the police. Detectives later said that Michael Ross behaved as if the police were his enemy and he was extremely careful not to show his true feelings during the interview.

One of Michael's classmates later said, 'Michael didn't trust anyone and, like his father, he wasn't impressed by other people. He and Eddy saw themselves as superior beings in many ways. No one was going to break Michael's spirit. He believed in his mission and was convinced he'd done nothing wrong.'

Michael Ross's interview with police detectives in the presence of his father produced absolutely nothing significant for the officers in charge of the case. Detectives were increasingly convinced Michael was the killer but the presence of his father Eddy had been unnerving for the police in many ways. Here was PC Eddy Ross, one of 'them' in a sense. Yet he was the one ensuring his own son, suspected of murder, did not say anything that might be held against him at a later date. While Eddy Ross may well have 'run' that first interview, he could not influence the detectives' strongly held opinion that his strong-willed teenage son had shot dead a man in cold blood. Detectives knew the biggest hurdle they would have to jump was Eddy Ross. As long as he was pulling the strings, these hard-working investigators would struggle to tie up the case.

At the end of the interview, Michael Ross shrugged his shoulders, got up and walked coolly out of the police station with a congratulatory pat on the shoulder from his father.

Inside the police station the two detectives, who had earlier been convinced that young Michael Ross would give them a fully blown confession, were stunned. They'd just let a teenage murder suspect walk free out of their police station and there wasn't a thing they could do to prevent it. Detectives now genuinely feared that this enquiry could crumble. Besides suspected 'killer' Michael Ross they also wanted to bring to justice his police officer father, whom they believed must have played an active role leading up to the killing at the very least. But how were they going to prove it?

Some of Michael Ross's classmates later recalled that Michael greatly enjoyed the notoriety of his alleged 'connection' to the murder. One said, 'Michael was positively beaming with pride. You could see it in his eyes if anyone asked him about it. He was the most famous pupil at the school by a mile. But some of us couldn't understand why he was still free.' A rumour went round Kirkwall grammar school that Eddy Ross had done a deal with his police friends to ensure Michael got off scot-free. It wasn't true but that wasn't the point.

# THE SNIPER'S STORY

The day after Michael Ross had been interviewed, on 25 September, police decided to grill the two friends whom Michael Ross claimed he met on the Eastabist on the evening of the murder. Neither of them could provide an alibi for Michael Ross. They completely denied meeting him. But there was a problem, because these witnesses were both fourteen years old and the circumstances behind their interviews with the police were questionable. Officers later admitted the statements were taken in the back of a police car with no appropriate adult present. And the handwritten statements, although signed by the children, were written by a police officer whose own handwriting was very hard to read. The forms hadn't even been properly signed.

The same day the BBC TV crew filmed their *Crimewatch* reconstruction of the murder at the actual crime scene. This understandably upset many locals out shopping because it re-ignited Orcadians' memories of the gun attack. As part of the show, a cameraman shadowed an actor playing the 'suspect' and other relevant characters around the town centre. Several witnesses also gave interviews to the BBC, who had set up camp in a court building in the middle of town. *Crimewatch UK* came in for a barrage of local criticism because the reconstruction was filmed in wet weather, the exact opposite of what it was like on the night of the actual murder. The idea behind the reconstruction was to jog people's memories but it simply didn't resemble the night in question, so how could it possibly work?

The devastating effect on the family of Shamsuddin Mahmood played second fiddle to the murder itself on *Crimewatch UK*. Bulbul Shafiuddin said from his Southampton home that his brother had no enemies and that the family had wanted him to get on with his studies rather than work as a waiter. But the saddest thing of all was, his brother told *Crimewatch UK*, that Shamsuddin Mahmood was aiming to return home to Bangladesh to marry his sweetheart.

DI Chisholm also appeared on the programme, appealing to *Crimewatch*'s millions of viewers for new information about the murder. The programme also featured an emotional interview with local businessman Donald Glue, who'd just sat down to eat with his wife and two young children when the killer walked into the Mumtaz, leaned across them and executed Mahmood. The father said, 'This has had such a serious effect on the family. There is a feeling of distrust now and none of us have hardly left the house since it happened.'

Some Orcadians later claimed *Crimewatch UK* made it too obvious that detectives believed the killer was a local man while not actually pointing the finger at Michael Ross. Also, said many in Kirkwall, why didn't the police mention any details about the weapon and bullets on the programme?

The programme was watched by an audience of ten million across the UK on 5 October 1994. The ripple effect was to heap even more pressure on police investigators. In the UK, police detection rates were supposed to be among the highest in the world. If that was the case, why had the killer not yet been apprehended? Some islanders genuinely believed that having the murder exposed on *Crimewatch UK* was bad publicity for the Orkneys in general and gave it the sort of 'fame' no one wanted. One Kirkwall resident pointed out, 'Those complaining completely missed the point of the programme. It wasn't about having a go at the Orcadians, it was about catching a killer.' Yet again certain locals were giving the impression that they didn't really care about the victim. They just didn't want outsiders prying into their business. 'It was typical and the fact the victim was black seemed to give certain bigoted Orcadians even more right to dismiss the importance of what had happened.'

Shortly after the show aired, an informant contacted the police to say that they thought they'd seen a man acting suspiciously near the public toilets close to the restaurant. The source didn't know the man's name, but jokingly mentioned that his military jacket most likely meant he was a soldier.

On 12 October, a Northern Constabulary firearms' department sergeant and a colleague carried out a brand new-arms test on all potential 9mm murder weapons on the Orkneys. This time these included the three 9mm pistols belonging to Eddy Ross, which hadn't been tested earlier. He'd steadfastly denied any of them worked and after stringent tests, police were satisfied that none of the weapons had been used to murder Shamsuddin Mahmood. But detectives knew only too well that someone as shrewd as Ross could easily have disposed of the murder weapon on behalf of himself and his son.

Around this time, detectives also established that Ross owned a total of eleven guns at the time of the murder – five pistols, two revolvers, three rifles and a shotgun – and they even heard he'd given son Michael a deactivated machine gun as a present. Both Michael and his younger brother Colin continued to be regularly taken out on shoots by their father. But none of this was enough to prove that Michael Ross was a murderer or that his father had helped cover up that crime. Detectives knew they needed to tread very carefully because these two were not normal, everyday criminals.

# 16.

ON 20 OCTOBER 1994, police were once again reminded of the diary belonging to murder victim Shamsuddin Mahmood, which they'd forgotten to pick up a few days after the killing back in June.

It had been rediscovered under the bed in the flat above the Mumtaz by one of the restaurant staff when he was tidying up the bedroom. No one mentioned at this time that the diary had first been offered to police immediately after the murder. The police were extremely fortunate to get another chance to see the diary, which would prove vital to their investigation because Mahmood had written every phone number and meeting he ever had in that diary.

Back at the Highlands police headquarters, more than a hundred and fifty miles away in Inverness, police bosses were demanding to know why the diary had been 'forgotten about' back at the start of the investigation. One detective admitted the error but insisted it did not have a bearing on the case. No wonder senior police officers in Inverness were getting increasingly concerned by the events unfolding in Kirkwall.

One former officer later said, 'The Inverness-based top brass were starting to look around for officers to blame for the enquiry's inability to make a significant arrest.'

The responsibility for the case had by this time been handed down to just two Inverness detectives still working fulltime in Kirkwall on the murder. They were supposed to be the 'experts' who'd crack the case but it was almost six months into the enquiry and they hadn't even managed to get a confession from a sixteen-year-old schoolboy. Behind the scenes, those same police chiefs were also suggesting that Eddy Ross might have been helped by other local Kirkwall officers 'sympathetic' to the Ross family.

Then, for the first time, detectives officially informed their bosses back in Inverness that the murder *was* racially motivated. The officers stated that many locals in the Kirkwall area had disliked the Bangladesh's working at the restaurant and these same folk were angry at police for continuing to build a case against Michael Ross. Some locals went on to seize on a new attempt to sell the Mumtaz restaurant by owner Moina Miah as irrefutable evidence that the murder was a contract killing by someone from outside. They also claimed that Mahmood was a gambler with debts and a drug dealer, as well as being the victim of a feud within the wider Bangladesh community, maybe even a womaniser who got his comeuppance. They also refused to accept that the motive behind Mahmood's shooting was racial hatred.

Many Orcadians thought they had reached a sad turning point. One said, 'We lost our innocence when that poor man died. People here suspected that racism lay behind the killing and we felt shamed by what had happened and the way that the killer was still on the loose.'

Another resident later said, 'It felt as if nothing would ever be the same again. A murder was bad enough but these other elements meant it affected just about everybody in the community in some way or other. Many were saying we would never shake off the implications. Orkney was no longer the beautiful, isolated paradise we had all thought it was. Beneath the surface there was hatred and prejudice just like everywhere else.'

In fact, the killing of Mahmood and the aftermath had frozen many Orcadians in a sense. They were unable to comprehend why the teenage son of a police officer some were saying was now the police's number-one suspect was still at liberty among them. How could the police not arrest him? many asked. Down south at police headquarters in Inverness, detectives were no longer even prioritising the case because they were swamped with day-to-day enquiries relating to other serious crimes committed on their patch. Also, detectives still hadn't even found the 9mm automatic used in the murder.

Meanwhile, road sweeper Jim Spence was trying to keep his head down and avoid any further conversations with Eddy Ross. Spence was stuck between a rock and a hard place. He wanted to tell the police the truth about that extra half-empty box of bullets but he was afraid of how Eddy Ross would react if he did. Detectives believed that Spence was the weak link but until he changed his story there was nothing they could do to pursue Ross any further.

Some weeks following his grilling by police, Michael Ross was at school when he bumped into the same girl he'd once boasted to about using his father's guns. Many of his classmates were by this time avoiding Michael because of rumours he was the killer of Shamsuddin Mahmood. The girl confronted Ross and pointed out that he'd told her he carried 'real' guns around regularly. Ross retorted that he didn't know what she was talking about but she later said as he spoke he had a chilling smile on his face.

Towards the end of November 1994, Jim Spence attended the funeral of an old friend from the British Legion. He should have realised that Eddy Ross would be there, too. This time Ross did not mention the bullets but he told Spence that police now had a definite suspect for the murder. Spence later recalled, 'Eddy said the man had lived in Kirkwall but that he'd disappeared after the murder and was now living rough somewhere in the hills behind the town.'

No doubt Ross had thought that by telling Jim Spence all this it might somehow lull him into believing that Ross was no longer suspected by police of involvement in the murder. But it actually had the opposite effect because it reminded nervous Jim Spence that the police must have worked out by now that he'd lied to them about the bullets.

Meanwhile, the two detectives still working full-time on the murder enquiry decided to go back to the drawing board. They carefully and discreetly collated every single piece of evidence they had that pointed to Michael Ross being the killer. The officers were extra-careful to make sure that any new enquiries did not alert any officers at Kirkwall police station just in case Eddy Ross got to hear about it. PC Ross was no doubt trying to go about his business as usual but it can't have been easy because half the town now knew his son was in the frame for the murder. But, typically, Eddy Ross kept his head held high and tried to make sure his problems at home did not in any way impact on his skills as a professional police officer.

# 17.

ON 2 DECEMBER 1994, Eddy Ross received a call from a colleague at the police station, saying there had been 'a development' in the hunt for the killer of Shamsuddin Mahmood and detectives wanted him and Michael to come in 'for a chat'.

As Eddy and his son were driving down to the police station from St Ola, a team of officers turned up at the family home overlooking Scapa Flow and began a painstaking search of the property. This revealed several significant finds, including a black balaclava with holes for eyes and mouth and that deactivated 9mm sub-machine-gun that Eddy had given his son and was found hanging on the wall of Michael Ross's bedroom. There was also a notebook belonging to Michael that had the two chevrons for corporal and the word 'Ross' written on it. This was the insignia with the 'o' of 'Ross' drawn with a swastika inside it and the two letters 's' looking like the Nazi SS emblem.

At the police station, Eddy Ross was asked by DI Chisholm to leave the interview room while his son was questioned about the Mahmood murder. Chisholm was perfectly within his rights to do this because Michael was now sixteen years old. Detectives then told Michael Ross they intended to record the interview under caution for a possible breach of the peace in relation to an alleged clash outside the Mumtaz two days before the murder, between Michael and Mahmood. This was crucial because detectives believed that this would put more pressure on Eddy Ross to come clean about everything.

Outside the room, Michael's father sat, stony-faced. He hadn't wanted to leave Michael alone with his police colleagues but perhaps he knew that in the long term this might prove an important part of both their defence strategies? During this second interview, Michael Ross also talked about his fight at the army cadet centre the day before the murder. He mentioned the damage to his knuckles and how his father Eddy took the minibus home that night. Although the detectives never once asked either father or son why Eddy Ross felt the need to do that. Michael mentioned being driven into town by his father the next morning and how he met two friends and eventually ended up shopping in the town centre until meeting his father at Woolworths and going home, leaving his brother Colin in Kirkwall.

Once again, Michael's overall demeanour was, detectives later recalled, very calm and cool for someone so young. It felt to detectives that Michael had been very carefully prepared for his interrogation. 'Michael remained composed throughout. He knew we wanted answers and he had plenty of them,' one police officer later recalled.

However, DI Chisholm then changed the approach he had used in the first interview back in September. He now recognised that this sixteen-year-old schoolboy had worked out how to 'play' the police when it came to interrogation. Chisholm firmly pressed Michael Ross to explain what happened in the woods:

| Michael Ross: | *Eh, [cough] well, I was up in the woods, eh, waiting for a boy. I was waiting there because, eh, he had been beating up one of my ex-girlfriends who I still fancied and, eh, I was going to give him a fright to, eh, stop him from hurting her again. [cough] That's why I was there anyway.* |
|---|---|
| DI Angus Chisholm: | *When you say you were going to give him a fright, what was your intention to do if you came across him that day?* |
| MR: | *Eh, I was, eh, going to pin him up a . . . pin him up, hold him by the throat, maybe, maybe give him a punch or two but then just go away.* |
| AC: | *Right, and this was over an ex-girlfriend of yours that he was now going out with was it?* |
| MR: | *Yeah.* |
| AC: | *OK. Did he come out that day?* |
| MR: | *No, he didn't.* |
| AC: | *What happened?* |
| MR: | *Eh, well, I realised that, eh, eh, he hadn't come out so I went off home again.* |
| AC: | *Right. So you weren't in school I take it that day?* |

MR:        *No I was eh, on study leave for exams.*

Ross even confirmed to detectives what clothes he had changed into and the green colour of the backpack he used that day. He also admitted having a balaclava with him, which he wore in the woods. It was black with three holes in it for eyes and mouth. He said he'd 'bought it down south' during a cadet training trip. Michael then astonished detectives by admitting that a few days after the murder he took the balaclava to school with him to show one of his friends.

That admission provoked a question from DI Chisholm.

AC:   *How? What would be the problem with having a balaclava in your bag?*
MR:   *Eh, eh, because a murder happening, eh, there're supposed to be a lot of kids and that going about, eh, frightening folk with them.*

Michael also admitted throwing two balaclavas away and mentioned during the interview that his father also had two balaclavas of his own. He said his mother had taken one of his tops and sold it at a jumble sale a few days after the murder. About halfway through the interview, DI Chisholm informed Ross that the story he told about his movements on the evening of the murder during his interview back in September did not stack up.

AC:   *Since that date we've spoken to the persons concerned and, eh, they don't, eh, corroborate the movements that you've given us, so what we've done*

*now is come back to ask you again to go over your*
*movements that night so we can be sure what*
*happened, eh, and make sure that there's no*
*mistakes or any there, OK?*

Michael Ross must have realised the two detectives were trying to nail him for the murder, but he remained just as calm as he'd been in that previous interview. He once again insisted he left the Eastabist estate on his bike for home at about 7.10 p.m. Ross told detectives he would have got home at 8.30 p.m. The officers immediately leaped on this, as it would never have taken so long for Michael to St Ola. For the first time that afternoon, Michael Ross seemed to have made a mistake. But then he backtracked and announced that he probably didn't leave town until about 8 p.m. instead of 7.10 p.m. DI Chisholm immediately reminded Michael Ross that his story had changed from his previous statement. Chisholm also reminded Michael Ross that two of the friends he had given as part of his alibi told the police they hadn't even seen Michael that night.

AC:     *So you can see how we are a bit concerned about*
        *what you're saying, you know?*

Michael Ross ignored the policeman's comments and insisted he did speak to them all. Then he stared challengingly into DI Chisholm's eyes.

AC:     *This is a bit of a problem for us, we would need to*
        *try and account for your movements that night in*
        *some way. Is there any way you can think of that*

> *somebody would account for where you were, is there*
> *anybody else you could have met, or spoken to?*

Michael Ross didn't respond this time.

One detective then drew a sketch map on which Michael identified the locations he claimed to have visited on the evening of the murder with a red felt-tip pen. After going over Ross's bike ride in great detail, the detectives decided it was time for a break, which left him hanging in the air, no doubt wondering what was coming next. A few minutes later the interview reconvened. This time DI Chisholm went in harder and immediately asked Michael Ross outright if he was in the vicinity of the murder scene that night.

AC:   *So were you anywhere near Bridge Street that night*
      *at all then?*

MR:  *No.*

AC:   *Do you know the man that was murdered?*

MR:  *No.*

AC:   *Have you ever met him?*

MR:  *Nuh.*

AC:   *Seen him?*

MR:  *I only seen him in the papers and that after the*
      *murder.*

AC:   *Have you ever been in the restaurant?*

MR:  *No, never been in the restaurant afore.*

AC:   *OK, I think that's it. I'll read this back and see if*
      *we've missed anything.*

The two detectives conducting the interview had presumed that once Michael Ross admitted being in the woods he'd then confess everything. But, in fact, he'd done the exact opposite. One former detective later said, 'It was crystal clear that Michael had been coached on what to say. It almost looks as if he was throwing a few bones at the detectives in the hope it would stop them from turning the thumb screws on him and Eddy.'

DI Chisholm later described the explanation given by Michael Ross as to his behaviour in Papdale Woods as a 'story'. He said that police checked and the boy that Michael had said he wished to confront had 'left the school, I think it was several months previous'. Michael Ross was released without charge.

An officer later said, 'The detectives had presumed that when Michael turned up with Eddy for the second interview without a solicitor it was a serious error on Eddy's part. Far from it, he knew that later on the fact that no solicitor was present might help to disqualify whatever evidence the police came up with and in turn that could convince a jury that his son was innocent.'

The police case against this father and son was weaker than ever.

# 18.

HAVING FAILED TO get a confession from Michael Ross, detectives decided it was time to focus on the 'bullet man' – Jim Spence. Then they could put together a proper case against Eddy Ross, as well as hopefully nailing his son for murder.

On 5 December detectives arrived unannounced at Jim Spence's small, shabby council home on the Eastabist and showed him a warrant to search the premises. Detectives said they were there because there had been a 'discrepancy' about the number of bullets that he gave to Eddy Ross.

DI Chisholm was polite but firm with Spence: 'D'you have you any objection to us searching your house, just to make sure that there's nothing else there, eh?'

Spence replied, 'I have an old slug gun, but it don't work, there's no trigger spring on it. I gotta rifle, it don't work, it ain't worked for years, sort of, something you should throw out but you don't, you just . . .'

Spence then stepped back as the officers began tearing his home apart. He must have been worried. However, he didn't want to be the one responsible for the arrest of either Eddy or Michael Ross. Spence later said he wished he'd never volunteered to talk to police in the first place and claimed his involvement with Eddy had 'ruined my life'. After the search was completed, Jim Spence was read his legal rights by police at home and later again at Kirkwall police station where he sat down for a full interview. Detectives made it clear that if he co-operated with them then he might be able to avoid jail time. This was followed by a recorded interview at the police station during which Jim Spence changed his story completely.

He stated that he'd given Eddy Ross a part-used box of the same type of 9mm Indian ammunition used in the murder. Spence was immediately charged with three offences. But this was all window-dressing as detectives had already indicated they would drop the charges in exchange for his evidence against Ross. Spence later insisted, under oath, that Ross asked him to lie about the stolen ammunition and branded his own motives for lying as 'a combination of dishonesty and self-interest'. After all, Spence had stolen the ammo, breached the Firearms Act and then lied to police during his first interview. He was also asked if he'd spoken to Ross recently. Spence took a deep breath and then revealed to detectives how Ross had approached him just a week earlier, at that friend's funeral. He finally came clean to detectives about the number of bullets he'd given to Eddy Ross. It appeared to be a significant turning point in the murder investigation.

Detectives believed they were finally closing in on their

'man' and would soon have him in custody. It was now time to haul him in yet again.

On the following afternoon, three police cars arrived at Kirkwall school. Officers made a high-profile arrest and word of Michael Ross's alleged role as the killer of Shamsuddin Mahmood soon spread through the town. This time detectives treated Ross more like an adult than a teenage schoolboy. However, his father was present on this occasion, although there was no solicitor at the interview. Detectives believed they had at last got the measure of both father and son.

One former officer later recalled, 'The Inverness detectives thought they had Michael by the short-and-curlies this time. They wanted Eddy to know they also had some dirt on him and those bullets. They fully expected to have the whole case down and dusted within hours.'

But it was not to be.

After hours of what one officer admitted was 'going round and round in circles' they had not established one significant new fact in the case against both men. 'Yet again the detectives presumed they'd crack both Eddy and Michael wide open. How wrong they were!' said a one-time Kirkwall police officer.

'By the end of six hours, the detectives looked more irritated than either of the Ross boys,' said an officer.

The mainland police had consistently misjudged the intelligence of the Rosses. This had now given Eddy and Michael an 'opening' in legal terms. Both father and son coped admirably with the mounting pressure. Detectives had no choice but to yet again release Michael Ross and his father.

One former associate of the Ross family later recalled, 'Eddy and Michael were on a high after that interview. They believed they'd won this battle and liked that feeling of invincibility. After all, if the cops still couldn't nail them for the Shamsuddin Mahmood murder then they would never be prosecuted, surely?'

DI Chisholm and his junior colleague from Inverness decided to take stock of the situation over Christmas. It certainly hadn't all gone according to plan but there had to be something they could pull out of the hat that would turn the case back in their favour.

* * *

At the start of the new year in 1995, murder detectives decided on one last throw of the dice, without telling any of their Kirkwall colleagues in advance, in case Eddy Ross got to hear what they were up to. On 5 January, police arrived at the Ross house in St Ola once again and this time officially arrested Michael Ross. He was encouraged to get legal representation. Detectives then informed Ross he would be attending an ID parade at Kirkwall police station that same morning. For the first time in months, Eddy Ross was lost for words. He'd not seen this one coming.

At the station, three unnamed witnesses who claimed to have seen a 'man' on the evening of the murder scrutinised a line-up of five men and were asked to identify the person they saw close to the scene of the murder. All three were understandably hesitant, so detectives encouraged them to take their time. Among the line-up, Michael Ross remained as calm as ever. Nothing about him stood out. After some minutes studying the men, none of the witnesses were able to positively identify Ross as being the person they saw that June evening the previous year. Afterwards, Ross family members and friends said it was 'hardly surprising' since all three witnesses had mentioned in statements that the man they saw was aged between twenty and thirty, and was not a (then) fifteen-year-old boy.

Eddy Ross was outraged by the identity parade and the way his son had been treated by police. He later said, 'Michael was placed in an identification parade in front of witnesses and nothing came of that . . . I never understood why this was done since the gunman was fully masked up.' As with so many things, Eddy Ross managed to make his outrage into something even more significant. 'I've been involved in many things in my life and experienced every possible emotion but at that particular time – the detention, house searching, accusations – it is difficult to describe the complete emptiness. I have looked after myself in many situations, my concern was for my family.'

Meanwhile, Scottish tabloid the *Daily Record* that same day publicly disclosed for the first time that Eddy Ross was suspected of trying to help cover up his son's alleged role in the murder of Shamsuddin Mahmood. Back at the police station, detectives led by DI Chisholm were once again reeling from yet another knockback in their investigation. While clearly infuriated that none of the three witnesses could identify Michael Ross as the killer, Chisholm was still determined not to let father or son off the hook. Three guns belonging to Eddy Ross were then confiscated by police, who alleged that he kept them unlicenced. But even this 'raid' fell at the first hurdle because Eddy Ross was able to prove once again that none of the weapons in question could be fired at all.

Detectives were by this time possessed of a sense of

injustice and gathered together every shred of evidence before submitting a detailed report on the case to the procurator fiscal (PF), the Scottish public prosecutor, in relation to the murder. But the application to charge Michael Ross was turned down flat. The PF did not feel the evidence was sufficient to achieve a guilty verdict.

'This didn't mean that Michael wasn't the killer in their eyes,' explained one former Orkneys officer. 'It just meant they hadn't gathered in enough proof to be certain of a prosecution.'

The police were hurting bad by this stage. They were privately infuriated by the way Eddy Ross seemed to be sneering at them once again following the prosecutor's refusal to charge his son with murder. Detectives turned their focus to the father. He certainly appeared to be a bad cop, the sort of person who could seriously damage the reputation of the police if he had been covering up for his son. One officer said, 'At least with Eddy, the guys in Inverness felt that they had more of a free reign to try and nail him . . . there was no point in pitter-pattering around, any more. The police were locked in a battle with one of their own and he was the sort of character who relished being in a fight. It undoubtedly empowered him and made him feel he was innocent.'

By the end of January, many residents of Kirkwall were even more concerned by the way the police were handling the murder case. One later said, 'The police chief, George Gough, originally leading the hunt, was back behind his desk in Inverness and other officers had also returned to the mainland. It felt as if they'd eased back even further on their enquiries, despite not arresting anyone for the murder. People started to wonder why.'

In fact, Detective Superintendent Gough had begun

making what were described in the local newspaper as 'flying visits' to the Orkneys to maintain some level of proactive involvement in the enquiry. On a number of occasions, he conducted new interviews and this alerted local newspapers hoping for a new angle on the story. But the media coverage nearly always ended with the same type of response from DS Gough: 'We are no nearer solving the case.'

Officers had taken more than 2,700 statements and checked nearly three thousand vehicles. Targeting Eddy Ross was a small consolation compared with bringing Michael Ross to justice.

# 19.

AT THE BRITISH Legion club just a couple of hundred yards from the Mumtaz restaurant, guns, bombs and bullets were an almost daily topic of conversation between members. No one was more engaged than club 'legend' Eddy Ross. He and the Legion remained the 'perfect fit'.

As an ex-soldier, Ross continued to consider it his duty to support and encourage vets from all the services to stick together. Some at the Legion found his forthright views a little polarising to say the least. But his undoubted ability to deliver a rousing speech had made him even more popular at the clubhouse in recent years. Stories about Ross's 'connection' to the bullet used to kill Shamsuddin Mahmood and how his teenage son could be the killer fell on relatively deaf ears in the clubhouse in the days and months following the shooting.

'No one ever asked Eddy about it,' one former member said. 'Even in the middle of all those interviews with the police, Eddy was at the club bright and early helping organise functions at the Legion.'

Many members interpreted his calm demeanour as further proof that he and his son were innocent of any involvement with the killing. 'Some members even implied that if his son had killed a complete stranger in cold blood it didn't really matter because his victim was black and of no importance to the community,' said one former member. Eddy Ross wasn't one for hiding from his community despite the gossip swirling around him. The same former member said, 'You'd think Eddy would have wanted to keep a low profile. But he made it clear his son hadn't done anything wrong – so why should he hide?'

Ross's told this author, 'I had and still have no reason to hide from anyone in Kirkwall. Why would I do such a thing? I have done nothing wrong.' Ross had no doubt that the British Legion was a much more honourable organisation than the Freemasons, who still included many serving and former police officers as members.

'Eddy hated the Freemasons even more after all this happened. I never quite understood why,' said a Kirkwall police officer. 'He seemed to see himself in competition with the Masons. It was all about power and influence and Eddy had that at the Legion while he was just another lowly copper at the Freemasons.'

At Kirkwall police station, some colleagues avoided all mention of Ross's alleged involvement with the bullet that killed Mahmood and the obvious implication that his own teenage son had committed the murder. 'It was a strange thing but many officers simply ignored it all,' said a retired officer. 'I think the officers from headquarters at Inverness found that frustrating, to say the least. Many of us stopped talking altogether about Michael and Eddy when we were at the station in Kirkwall because we suspected that certain officers might tip Eddy off if there were any plans to grill him again.'

No doubt Ross's continued employment as a police officer in Kirkwall was hard to swallow for many of his colleagues, who felt he should have at least been suspended following the exposure of his alleged connection to the Mahmood case. In fact, Eddy had been allowed to continue serving as a police officer in Kirkwall in the belief that this might make him think he was no longer under suspicion, prompting him to let his guard slip. But Ross was a canny character who saw himself and his son as completely innocent of all alleged crimes and he'd worked out what was happening.

As the cold, wet, winter months gradually gave way to the spring of 1995, murder squad detectives back in Inverness decided it was time to take the battle to Eddy's doorstep. They could not bear the idea of letting both father and son off the hook. On 13 March, Eddy was hauled into his boss's office in the station and told he was to be suspended on full pay until the Shamsuddin Mahmood enquiry team had concluded their investigations and either cleared Eddy and his son or charged either or both of them. Friends and associates of Ross later said he took the news in remarkably good spirits. One later said, 'Eddy was supremely confident that neither he or Michael would be found guilty of anything. As he always said, he had nothing to hide.'

However, behind the scenes, Ross was growing increasingly resentful towards the police in general. He would later claim that some of his Kirkwall colleagues simply wanted to clear up the Mahmood murder case and that he, Eddy, and his son were 'convenient targets'. Many years after the events, he told this author, 'I simply don't trust the police after what happened. It's a shame because I was once one of them but now I realise how inefficient and dishonest some of them can be. It's a tragedy but it's the truth.'

Ross felt the finger of suspicion hanging over him from the moment news of his suspension from Kirkwall police leaked out. It must have felt to him as if he was a marked man. Later, he admitted that his suspension had a highly adverse effect on his family in general. It also caused problems with his son Michael. As Eddy later explained, 'I was furious with Michael. I shouted at him a lot at the beginning. We were all under incredible pressure.' But gradually father and son rebuilt their tight bond and Ross told family and friends he was convinced that he and Michael had been framed by his former police colleagues.

At his beloved British Legion clubhouse, Ross's suspension from work as a police officer was met with derision in some quarters. 'Most of us thought it was a bloody joke,' one member of the Legion said. 'How could they suspend a man from work when they hadn't even got enough evidence to arrest him? We all felt sorry for Eddy and most of us were convinced neither him or Michael had done anything wrong.'

The one silver lining for Eddy Ross and his family at this time was that he had been suspended on full pay, so they wouldn't suffer financially. At the Legion clubhouse bar, many members nodded in agreement with Ross when he said it was all a huge mistake. 'They had no actual evidence, so they did the next best thing and pushed the poor man out of the door,' said one Legion member.

While his father had his refuge at the Legion clubhouse, Michael Ross was spending more and more time on the Eastabist council estate, even though Eddy warned him to be extremely careful about whom he discussed the murder case with. Eventually, father convinced son that he was 'safer' at home and pulled away from all his council estate friends in case any of them made allegations about him to the police. Eddy Ross eventually began to look on his suspension as a challenge created for him by mainland police. He knew what their game was and he decided that he was going to carry on as if nothing whatsoever had happened.

One former officer said, 'The problem was that Kirkwall is such a small place. I'd bump into Eddy all the time and, quite frankly, sometimes I'd duck down a side road to avoid him because he was someone you just didn't want to be connected with at that time. There was a feeling among most of us in Kirkwall that the police in Inverness needed to take this pair by the scruff of the neck and sort the case out once and for all. It would be much easier for them to do that than us.'

The Kirkwall population – many of whom knew Eddy Ross personally – was still very much split down the middle. One Kirkwall resident later said, 'Some of the more traditional citizens – many of whom belonged to clubs like the British Legion – became even more vocal about how the police should lay off Eddy and Michael because they were innocent. But most disturbing of all, some of these same characters were being even more open about how the victim was just a black waiter of no consequence so it didn't even matter that he'd died.'

Meanwhile, there was an ever growing feeling of resentment between the police in Kirkwall and the detectives down south in Inverness. One former officer said, 'The

Inverness police were piling on pressure on us to watch Eddy's every move but it wasn't easy because he knew we were on him and he was extremely careful to watch his back. Eddy did absolutely nothing wrong in the months following his suspension and many of us started wondering if maybe he *was* innocent after all. Perhaps his son had committed the murder using bullets he stole from his father but that didn't necessarily make Eddy guilty.'

At one stage, a two-man 'team' of local police officers were 'encouraged' by their colleagues in Inverness to visit all Eddy's friends and acquaintances to try and gather more evidence against him. 'It was clumsy and of course Eddy soon knew all about it,' said one of Eddy Ross's former colleagues. 'It also made us feel used by the Inverness police. They didn't seem to care how awkward this all was for us.' This resentment between the so-called 'city boys' from Inverness and their 'country bumpkin cousins' from Kirkwall was especially helpful to Eddy Ross because it slowed down the entire investigation.

Obviously, no one exactly knows how Eddy Ross felt at this time except Eddy himself but there was a feeling in Kirkwall that the longer police did not charge him the more likely he was to be cleared of all accusations and reinstated as a police officer. 'And the murder itself was starting to fade in people's memories,' said one Legion member. 'Even if Michael was the killer none of us thought he was a danger to anyone else and most of us just wanted the police to give up and leave us all in peace.'

In response to this, Chief Constable Bill Robertson flew in from Inverness and made a whistle-stop appearance in Kirkwall to try and allay fears that the enquiry had ground to a halt. But his visit did little to quell the anger and disappointment felt by many in the community, even after Robertson issued a public statement asking the local community to be patient with the progress of the investigation because he was hoping some arrests would occur soon. Some police officers believed that Eddy Ross was the sort of father who'd make sure his son never made such a colossal mistake ever again. One former police officer said, 'A lot of us felt that Eddy was protecting his son come what may. It's a tricky one for any parent. You want to help your child, even if he's done something really bad.'

Another detective said many years later, 'We all knew what sort of father Eddy was. He'd make sure Michael never got off the leash ever again. But Orcadians talked about Michael as if he was nothing more than a troublesome teenager, rather than a suspected homicidal maniac.'

One Kirkwall resident later insisted, 'Suspending Eddy and then waiting for him to crack was a pathetic attempt by the police to solve the murder and it was far too little, too late. We didn't want insincere words from the police. We wanted action. That killer was still out there and the police were no closer to catching him.'

Others in the community had a more cynical outlook. One said, 'A lot of us had heard Michael Ross's name being linked to the killing and we started to wonder if the police were easing off their enquiries on the basis that Michael was of no further threat.'

Many Orcadians believed neither father or son would ever pay for their crimes.

# 20.

ON 3 AUGUST 1995, murder detectives searched the underground sewers beneath the central streets of Kirkwall to see if the killer of Shamsuddin Mahmood had used them to make his escape on the night of the murder.

The police focused on one particular pipe that ran from Junction Road all the way to Papworth Woods. But after hours of examination, they concluded that no one had used it as an escape route.

Having suspended Eddy Ross from his job earlier in the year, detectives were now giving the impression they'd run out of leads relating to him and his son. But, in fact, they'd actually revived their interest in Michael Ross. A number of secret interviews were carried out with some of his friends, those who had originally been approached by police officers the previous year. These individuals were all given secret police codenames because there was a genuine fear they might end up being intimidated by supporters of the Ross family.

Some of those witnesses helped police build a picture of

Michael Ross that indicated he was a loner prepared to fight with anyone whom he didn't like. Officers put together a timeline that showed the build-up to the Mahmood murder and how Michael had been behaving very erratically in the days and weeks leading up to the killing.

On 24 August, Inverness's DI Chisholm requested what in Scottish law is called a petition warrant to arrest Michael Ross for the murder. He handed over a package of evidence to the district fiscal prosecutor in Inverness. But the prosecutor refused to refer the case. The police were astonished. They'd been knocked back by authorities yet again. One Orcadian resident later agreed, 'We were stunned. We believed the police knew exactly what both father and son had done but the prosecutor was preventing them from doing their job properly.'

Around this time, Shamsuddin Mahmood was finally buried back in his home country of Bangladesh. By this time one of his younger brothers had set up a school scholarship in Mahmood's name and the family hoped that the funeral might help them start to rebuild their lives. However, there was a growing resentment about the failure of the police to bring anyone to justice for the cold blooded killing of their beloved family member.

Meanwhile, at the Ross family home on the hills above historic Scapa Flow, Eddy was no doubt delighted when Michael assured him that he still planned to sign up for his beloved Black Watch regiment as soon as he left school in the following summer. It had been many months since Eddy's suspension from his job as a PC and yet Inverness detectives still hadn't found enough new evidence to arrest Eddy, either.

'The police in Inverness were growing very frustrated,' said one former Kirkwall officer. 'Some of them were privately accusing the police in Kirkwall of protecting the Ross family. It was a stupid thing to say because Eddy was far from popular. Sure, there might have been a couple of old school coppers who stuck up for Eddy and Michael but the rest of us had little doubt about Eddy's involvement. However, we had to face Eddy and his family in Kirkwall town centres most days and we certainly weren't going to falsify evidence in order to help the police in Inverness prosecute a guy who'd worked alongside us for many years.'

With the relationship between Kirkwall police and the mainland detectives now at an all-time low, senior officers on both sides tried to end the stalemate by agreeing a 'peace treaty' to try and mend the broken fences between the two units. One former Orkneys officer said, 'The atmosphere was so bad between us that the fact we were both supposed to hunting a killer got lost in a sense. It was really bad. We all needed to look at ourselves and stop squabbling like children and get back to the task at hand.'

* * *

In the early summer of 1996, Michael Ross, aged seventeen, joined the Black Watch regiment just as his father had wished. Michael could forget all about the rumours and implications that had swirled around him for the previous two years. Eddy later confirmed that he was relieved that Michael – still a murder suspect – was away training with the regiment at Fort George, an imposing seventeenth-century artillery building located at the mouth of the Moray Firth near Inverness. It had originally been built specifically to quench the Jacobite cause in the Highlands following the failed attempt to seize the throne by Bonnie Prince Charlie in 1745–56.

Everything about Fort George – named after King George II – was built on a grand scale, with an outer boundary wall stretching over a mile in circumference. Inside the bristling defences were quarters for over 1,600 soldiers, with further accommodation for officers, a fort governor, and an artillery detachment. Aside from residential housing, there were extensive armouries, including a magazine made to hold more than 2,500 barrels of gunpowder.

Over the previous few years the Black Watch had maintained a presence in dozens of different countries. The regiment prided itself on training hard for their peacekeeping operations, while at the same time maintaining a conventional capability that upheld the reputation of the regiment.

Michael Ross quickly settled into life with his new 'family'. At Fort George there was a reveille call every morning on a bugle with a piper playing 'Johnnie Cope' to rouse the soldiers at the start of another day. The Black Watch centered its ethos around honour, gallantry and devoted service to monarch and country. Battles that contributed most to Black Watch history ranged from Fontenoy to Ticonderoga, Waterloo and El Alamein.

Back in St Ola and Kirkwall, suspended police officer PC Eddy Ross continued to appear in the community as if he had nothing to hide – and in his mind, as ever, this remained the case. Friends and family were saying it was about time the police admitted they were wrong and reinstated him in the post he so adored. Eddy himself wrote to the crown prosecutor's office asking what was going on. He was pushing for a decision to drop the charges. This infuriated the police and prosecutors. But would it backfire on Eddy Ross?

# Part Three

# Justice?

'If we can't deal with the past how on earth can we have a future?'
– Kirkwall resident

# 21.

IN MARCH 1997– two years after his initial suspension –
Eddy Ross found his life turned upside down when he was
charged with concealing important evidence connected to the
murder of Shamsuddin Mahmood.

The indictment against Ross also stated that he was charged
with possession of an unlicenced handgun. He claimed he
had the gun to protect himself and his family after rumours
of his and Michael's connection to the murder began to leak
out in Kirkwall. The indictment also named various men
Ross was alleged to have worked with to help him cover up
the murder between the day of the murder on 2 June and
the end of 1994. Ross was also alleged to have asked road
sweeper Jim Spence to lie to officers about the quantity of
the ammunition he had earlier received from him. During a
brief appearance at Kirkwall magistrates court Eddy Ross was
immediately granted bail. This clearly indicated he was not
considered a flight risk. Ross himself no doubt believed that

being out and about in Kirkwall would undoubtedly help his case because he'd hardly do such a thing if he was guilty, would he?

Newspapers and TV news led on the arrest but were unable to expand on the background to the case for legal reasons. Reading a story about how the policeman father of a murder suspect was alleged to have 'interfered' with evidence was enough to whet many peoples' appetites to learn much more. Ross was referred by magistrates to appear two months later at Inverness high court to face the charges, which also included one of wilful neglect and violation of his duty after being alleged to have concealed evidence from senior police detectives Detective Superintendent George Gough and Detective Inspector Angus Chisholm.

Ross's trial commenced in a blaze of publicity with dozens of journalists jostling for seats in the press area and a full public gallery at the high court. Typically, Eddy Ross himself seemed calm and even had an air of indifference about it all. But he must have feared doing anything that would contribute to bringing the case against his son into public awareness. Michael had never been charged and Eddy wanted to avoid the allegations against his son damaging the young man's career with the Black Watch regiment. Arriving at court every day to face all this attention, Eddy Ross wore a flat cap and was expressionless throughout. But he looked a lot older than his forty-six years.

In the dock, Ross had to endure the court hearing evidence that he had hindered, delayed and frustrated the investigation into the shooting and that he had therefore attempted to defeat the ends of justice (the Scottish equivalent of the offence of perverting the course of justice). The police insisted that Ross had concealed from them the total amount of 9mm ammunition given to him twenty years earlier by former marine Jim Spence. Then on 22 May, DI Chisholm took the witness stand and insisted to the court that Eddy Ross was not and never had been a suspect in the murder. Defence lawyer Herbert Kerrigan asked DI Chisholm: 'The situation is that at some point later suspicion focused on Mr Ross's son, is that correct?'

Eddy Ross's heart must have sunk at this moment. Michael was being linked to the murder in open court. DI Chisholm then informed the court that Michael Ross had not been eliminated from inquiries, despite some media outlets believing that was the case. When defence barrister Mr Kerrigan suggested to the court that an identification parade had eliminated Ross's son from the inquiry, DI Chisholm replied, 'No, that's not correct.'

Kerrigan asked, 'Did it confirm he was there?'

Chisholm had to admit Michael Ross was not picked out at the parade.

The defence then suggested the only evidence relating to Ross's son was the killer wearing a balaclava and Michael admitting being in a local wood wearing a similar balaclava. Chisholm told the court that was not correct. Kerrigan then asked the detective what other evidence there was in relation to Ross's son and the murder.

Chilsholm replied, 'Eddy Ross's son's alibi at the time of the murder cannot be confirmed. It is confirmed as being incorrect. He is also of a similar appearance to the person who walked into the restaurant.'

No doubt Eddy Ross had presumed such a damning statement could not be made in open court. But the judge,

Lord MacLean, allowed the reporting of the evidence after prosecutor James Campbell QC said there were no proceedings pending in the murder inquiry into the killing of Shamsuddin Mahmood. Ironically, Ross's arrest and prosecution had enabled lawyers to openly name Michael as chief suspect in the murder. Ross had no doubt looked on himself as his son's protector, prepared to take on all-comers to help Michael fight what he described as 'the false charges'. But his trial had been used to publicly accuse Michael of murder. It was a pivotal moment in the trial because Michael's alleged role in the killing also meant that Eddy Ross's innocence would be much harder to prove.

Ross spent his last weekend before the jury went out at his St Ola home. Moira hadn't attended the court at all because she had to look after the couple's two other children, including a ten-year-old daughter. In the early hours of a misty Monday morning at the end of June, Ross gave his wife and children a hug, and headed off to the tiny airport just outside Kirkwall to fly down to Inverness to hear the decision of the court. Ross steadfastly maintained his innocence and told his family he expected to be back home very soon.

A few hours later, Eddy Ross was found guilty of deliberately hindering investigations into the murder and sentenced to four years' imprisonment.

He later claimed that after his sentencing he was taken into a side room at the court and one of the prosecuting solicitors admitted he was shocked by the guilty verdict. Moments later, two police officers escorting Eddy Ross insisted that he removed his tie in accordance with the rules following a conviction. Eddy Ross told them he would resist any attempt to do this. Ross later claimed both officers backed down and let him keep his tie on. But there was more humiliation to come for the one-time police constable. The van taking him to nearby Porterfield prison was not backed right up to the rear exit to the building, which was the convention allowing convicted criminals to step straight into the van.

'But the van stopped short so I had to go into the yard,' Ross said. Thirty feet away from where he stepped out were banks of photographers snapping away. 'I knew who had set this up. They saw me as a policeman who had done wrong and they were making an example of me.'

Back in Kirkwall, some immediately proclaimed that Eddy Ross had been 'stitched up'. 'It felt to some of us as if Eddy was taking the heat for Michael by facing his accusers in court while his son was mapping out a career as a professional soldier,' said one resident.

Moira Ross – still working as a nurse in the cancer ward of Kirkwall's East bank hospital – called Michael at his barracks immediately after the verdict was given and later said Michael was 'devastated' by the news. Ross was furious about his family's treatment. He was particularly upset that Moira had heard the news of his four-year prison sentence via a news broadcast and not through his former colleagues. Ross had expected the police to visit their house to tell her the court's verdict, or at least send a welfare officer. But no one bothered. He also pointed out over and over again that there was – as had earlier been revealed in court – no forensic evidence against his son and no link between Michael, himself and the murder victim.

Ross said, 'They knitted two things together [the bullets and Michael with the balaclava] and you have a beautiful stew. If you look at it from their point of view and the way it is presented in court, I would have found myself guilty.'

After Ross's conviction, Mahmood's brother Bulbul Shafiuddin told journalists he feared that the investigation into the actual murder would fade away. He and his family were still outraged that no one had been prosecuted for the killing itself. 'I definitely think there should be some kind of inquiry,' Shafiuddin told one reporter, 'but always at the back of my mind is whether there will be justice.' The fact that Michael was a serving soldier shocked the victim's family because they'd presumed he would not have been allowed to join the army while he was under suspicion. Shafiuddin also felt guilt-ridden after his brother had settled in the UK after staying with him in Southampton. 'If I had never brought him here he would have remained alive today. It did not occur to me that I would have to bring his dead body home.'

The family also believed the inability to charge let alone find anyone guilty of the murder proved the Scottish justice system suffered from the same kind of institutional racism highlighted in the Macpherson report, which followed up the trial of the alleged racist killers of black teenager Stephen Lawrence in south London in 1993. 'I want to see justice,' Shafiuddin said following Eddy Ross's conviction. 'It's not because he is our brother but because it is in the greater interest of the country.'

* * *

Eddy Ross's new home for the next few years was Porterfield prison, near Inverness. It had been designed more than a hundred years earlier to house 104 inmates. But through the decades it had become grossly overcrowded and had for many years been lacking in decent living conditions, according to many former inmates. Porterfield achieved worldwide notoriety in the 1970s after Glasgow gangster Jimmy Boyle and Howard Wilson – a former police officer who shot two former colleagues dead after a robbery – were kept in specially built steel cages to prevent rioting. Those same cages were dismantled only a few months before Ross became an inmate at the same jail. Many prison staff believed the cages should have stayed because they acted as a big deterrent to troublesome inmates.

If Ross had served his sentence at Porterfield in the 1970s, he might not have come out alive. Back then bloody riots, battles and disturbances were almost daily occurrences, as they had been at many other Scottish prisons at that time. There was one good thing about Porterfield prison from Ross's perspective: by the time he arrived it was once more a relatively small prison with just over one hundred inmates. This meant Ross could make his presence felt to both inmates and staff.

Initially, he was kept in solitary confinement for – prison staff claimed – his own safety because he was a policeman. But Ross hated being kept in what was referred to as the 'kiddy-fiddler' (child molester) wing of the prison because of the nature of the offences committed by many of the inmates around him. He had always been a traditional crime-and-punishment-style copper during his twenty-year career with the police service in the Orkneys. But now he was seeing life from the other side. But Ross wasn't scared of anyone and considered himself innocent of all the charges. He demanded to be allowed to mix with the general prison population. Ross's wish was eventually granted and he was soon telling fellow inmates that he'd been fitted-up (framed) because his one-time police colleagues were out to get him.

This gritty, defiant attitude must have endeared him to many inmates, a lot of whom made similar claims to anyone who would listen.

In some ways, Eddy was thriving in his new home while in the outside world many were paying a much heavier price for the Ross family's alleged involvement in a cold-blooded murder.

# 22.

WITH HER HUSBAND now facing four years behind bars and her oldest son named as the number one suspect in a murder, Moira Ross broke her self-imposed silence and decided it was time to speak out.

The trial of Eddy had shaken the Ross family to the core. Moira was so upset she agreed to give her first-ever press interview after being door-stepped by a *Daily Record* reporter at the family's home the day after Eddy's sentencing. As far as Moira Ross was concerned both her husband and son were innocent. She told the tabloid, 'My son's no killer. It's totally shattered our lives. I haven't a clue where I'm going to go from here. I'm feeling devastated.' She insisted she didn't even know when she'd next see Eddie. 'I just don't know. We all love him so much.' But she had talked on the phone since the verdict. She told the reporter, 'He's as well as can be expected.' However, Moira was shocked by how defeated her husband sounded during the call although, typically, he'd urged Moira and his children to cope as best they could. 'There's no justice at all. I hope to appeal and hopefully something will come of that.'

Following Ross's sentencing, his elderly mother wrote to local newspaper the *Orcadian* protesting his innocence. Ross himself refused to admit his involvement in the alleged crimes. And back in the tiny hamlet of St Ola there still wasn't a soul who thought either Eddy or Michael were guilty of involvement in any aspect of the murder of Shamsuddin Mahmood.

Despite his shock at that guilty verdict, Eddy Ross dusted himself down and got on with the next adventure of his life, as a prison inmate. Once they got to know him, Eddy Ross was treated with the utmost respect by the Porterfield prison staff, from the governor down. He was even given specialist duties such as working in the library and as an office assistant to the senior staff at the prison. Eventually, Ross was allowed twice a week to leave the prison to carry out maintenance on a local sea cadet centre. He also accompanied the deputy governor on a number of outside events as well as being encouraged to attend college three days a week to study law. This type of treatment simply reinforced Eddy's belief that his verdict was a farce, a complete travesty of justice.

Some believed that Eddy Ross actually quite enjoyed his time in prison because it wasn't that dissimilar to being in his beloved army. Ross thrived on discipline and soon worked out how to play the system. Many he encountered were bewildered by his good manners and grace under pressure and few could put a label on him because the offences he'd been accused of were so unusual. One former inmate who knew him said, 'What you saw was what you got with Eddy. He never flinched. He was immaculately turned out every day. But most important of all he never looked scared of anyone, and inside prison that is the key to surviving in one piece.' Ross's adjustment to prison life astonished everyone from his closest friends and associates back in Kirkwall to the murder squad detectives who were responsible for his incarceration. 'I remember one time, Eddy helped out a young inmate who could hardly read and write by writing a letter to his family for him. He didn't do it to impress anyone. He did because he considered it his duty to help those who were less well off than him.'

Ross clearly had the ability to step back from his difficult predicament and patiently work through his sentence, knowing full well that his family and friends would still be there for him when he got out. But back home in St Ola, Moira no doubt struggled to cope with her husband's incarceration as she brought up their two other children. Meanwhile, police and at least some local people hoped the publicity generated by Ross's trial would flush out the killer, whom most believed to be Michael. Top Inverness investigator DS Gough told reporters, 'We hope that somebody may have heard something at the trial that will jog their memory.'

In prison, Ross had plenty of time to think about his and his family's predicament. He remained convinced that his own case was motivated by political expediency. He bemoaned the fact they couldn't find the killer so they tried for the next best thing – a so-called bent cop. 'I know how this works, I'm not stupid. I've seen so many things like this happen. Once the wheels are in motion you can't stop it, even if you wanted to,' he told one newspaper reporter, briskly. Referencing the way in which he had entered the restaurant after the murder and the allegation that he hadn't been invited, he commented, 'During my trial one cop said I had, more or less, persuaded myself in to the scene of crime. Absolute no-no. No one enters unless they are invited in – the lowest cop or the chief constable. There was no way I would have walked in.'

Typically, Eddy's long-standing gallows humour kicked in while he was in prison. He even joked to other inmates about how he and his family 'usually sit around polishing our Kalashnikovs'. Despite everything, Eddy could see the funny side of things, although none of it had been a laughing matter for innocent murder victim Shamsuddin Mahmood.

In his cell at night Eddy must have gone through the facts of the case over and over in his mind as well as scribbling notes down in an exercise book. He saw his incarceration as this: 'What did I do? I was honest. I was sentenced for being honest.'

Eight months into his prison sentence, Ross officially resigned from the Northern Constabulary. He did it in advance of a police disciplinary hearing that was then shelved before it could reveal any more evidence against him. Ross had originally planned to retire in 1999, at the age of forty-nine, after completing twenty-five years of police service. Now that pension would have to be put on ice until he was sixty because of his criminal record.

Some close to the Ross family later insisted that Michael Ross felt extremely bad about not being a stronger supporter to his father during and just after his trial. But Ross had insisted Michael stay away because he didn't want his son pulled to pieces in the media. And as a result, Michael ensured that his new found passion for the Black Watch regiment never faltered. It was the least he owed his father. Michael wrote letters to his father and even visited him a couple of times with his mother Moira.

Back at his army base at Fort George, Michael rarely let his mask slip. But he was irritated when another young soldier serving alongside him won the first marksman competition he took part in with the Black Watch regiment. Michael didn't like coming second to anyone. But it was his extraordinary ability to cut himself off emotionally that astonished so many people who met him at this time. His own father was in prison for helping him avoid a murder charge and yet Michael's face never changed expression, even when he watched TV reports of the case. Some would describe that ability to cut off emotionally as an example of good, professional soldiering. Others saw it differently. They felt that Ross had developed this chilling ability to completely lack empathy with anything that got in the way of his progress in life.

In Porterfield, model inmate Eddy Ross's prison career as a clerical assistant was going from strength to strength. Officers were convinced he would never make any attempt to escape. One former member of staff at Porterfield later said, 'Eddy made it clear he would serve his time, even though he was innocent. I think it was his army background that made him that way.' Soon Eddy was even running errands for the prison governor's office.

An inmate said, 'There was no question of dishonesty when it came to Eddy. Eddy was a highly efficient, intelligent character and the prison staff recognised this and rewarded his good behaviour with some of the best jobs inside prison.'

But others inside the Porterfield got a different impression of Ross. One former inmate remembered, 'There were times when Eddy acted more like a mobster than a copper when he was inside. His presence terrified a lot of the other inmates and staff. People bowed down to him as if he was some kind of God. It was ridiculous.'

And – as with most prisons across the globe – there was a pecking order to be observed. No wonder some of the smaller, weaker characters looked up to Ross as if he was some kind of demigod. The same former inmate explained: 'If he'd wanted to, Eddy could have run that prison single-handedly. And naturally, Eddy never knowingly broke the law while he was inside.' Ross must have been steadfastly determined to prove to the world he was an honest, honourable man wrongly imprisoned for something he had not done.

Eventually, he was allowed out of prison to attend staff functions. Many years later, Ross himself told this author how he was offered a glass of wine to drink at one such event. He said, 'I refused that alcoholic beverage and pointed out that as a serving inmate alcohol was strictly prohibited and I had no intention of breaking the rules.' Despite being in prison, Ross remained a stickler for rules and regulations, which of course his two sons knew only too well. But then Ross had once told a colleague, 'Discipline. That's the key word when it comes to this world. If people kept to the rules and did exactly what they should, then we'd all be living in a much happier place.'

But, typically, Ross was careful not to share *all* his opinions with his fellow inmates. He was extremely careful not to talk about the charges he'd faced apart from saying he was innocent. One inmate later said, 'Eddy knew what to expect inside prison. He knew that for every "nice" inmate there was another one ready to stitch you up to the coppers if you said anything that they might be able to use against you. I remember one time – Eddy had a crowd of inmates round him in the yard and they were all firing questions at him about what had happened to that waiter in Kirkwall. One inmate asked Eddy if it was true that his son was the number one suspect for the murder of the waiter. Well, Eddy stopped in his tracks when he heard that question, looked at the man who asked it – right in his eyes – then turned around and walked away from the group without saying another word.

'The other inmates had a right go at this other man. They told him to leave Eddy in peace. I realised then that many of them were in awe of Eddy. He had them all under his spell in a sense.'

About a year and half into his sentence, Eddy Ross found himself on a boat trip on Loch Ness. It was something he laughed about many years later when he met this author. 'Yes, that Loch Ness trip was true. I was part of the governor's staff that day. They took me along because I'd never ever tried to escape or do anything illegal in prison. I was trusted and expected to be trusted because I wasn't like most of the other inmates.'

But there was one 'disciplinarian' issue that was threatening his chances of an early release from prison. Many years later he revealed, 'I refused point-blank to admit to my crimes and there is an unwritten rule in the prison service that says an inmate must do this in order to be granted early release and probation.' Ross refused to 'admit' his crimes because he'd convinced himself he hadn't done anything wrong. 'How could I admit sorrow for something I never did?' he said to one journalist. 'It was outrageous to expect me to confess all and I was determined to stick to my guns.' As a result of this dispute an impasse existed between Ross and the prison probation service for some months. He later said, 'They knew I would never apologise because I believed I had done nothing wrong.'

Ross even accepted that his alleged 'insubordination' was most likely going to lead to him to serve the maximum time in prison. One former colleague said, 'But Eddy wouldn't back down on the issue. He stuck to his guns. That was typical of him.'

Yet somewhere inside the machine that ran Scottish prisons at that time, someone decided that despite Ross's refusal to admit to his crimes he should be released early because he was no threat to anyone on the outside. Just before the second anniversary of his incarceration, Ross was informed he would be released imminently. He later told this author, 'That proves my point entirely. They were telling me I'd have to serve the full four years unless I admitted to my crimes. But they still let me out early.' And, typically, Ross had another big surprise awaiting his probation officer on his release. 'Having been informed I would be released, my probation officer said to me, "You won't be going back to Kirkwall I presume?" I was appalled. Why on earth wouldn't I go back to my home town?' Ross said that he had nothing to be ashamed of and he had no intention of running away by going to live somewhere else. 'My family, my friends were all there,' he later said, 'but the probation officer seemed to think that I might upset a lot of folk by being there. Nonsense.'

His self-belief was as strong as ever. A fellow inmate later said, 'That's a measure of the man. You can't help respecting someone who refuses to bow down to the system. He stood by his own beliefs and in the end they had to let him out early.'

Nothing would stop Eddy Ross from returning home to where he had lived for so much of his adult life. He was proving once again he was not scared of anyone. His arrival back in St Ola was greeted by a welcome home party attended by more than thirty neighbours, friends and family. Ross was very touched and reassured that so many people still believed in him. He told those at the party, 'I'm glad of this support, from my wife and family and all those from the neighbours.'

Other Kirkwall residents were not quite so enthusiastic about Eddy Ross's return to the community. One later said, 'The stories about Eddy and, even more importantly, Michael's involvement with the murder of Shamsuddin Mahmood had continued swirling around the islands. Yet here was Eddy back among us acting as if nothing whatsoever had happened. He didn't seem any different from before he went to prison. He was polite to everyone but there was always this steely look in his eyes. It was a look of determination and pride. It was as if Eddy was saying to all of us, "Come on, come and get me".'

'But of course none of us wanted to "get" Eddy. We just wanted the person who murdered Shamsuddin Mahmood in cold blood to be dealt with. And until that crime was solved there was this strange air of fear hanging over Kirkwall, even though some years had now elapsed since the murder.'

And the very next day after his return home, Eddy Ross could be seen out in the town centre, head held high as he visited numerous shops with wife Moira. One fellow resident later said, 'I suppose Eddy was saying, "I'm back", as if nothing had happened.'

This was not entirely the case. As far as Ross was concerned, there was a lot of unfinished business to attend to. He was soon planning the next stage of his family's battle with the authorities, including those murder detectives from the mainland who'd cost him two years of his life in prison. Everywhere he went, he made sure to say what he thought of his treatment by the police. 'It was a joke,' he told one local newspaper reporter. He also directed his anger at the amount of pre-publicity his trial had received and how it must have been prejudicial to his case. And he publicly questioned the credibility of two police witnesses at his original trial. He said, 'If you're giving a statement, it has to be positive of what you saw, not words like "maybe" or "possibly", you want people to be firm or sure. A serving police officer's statement was full of "maybes", "I am not sure", "possibly". To me that was a statement that should never have been put forward.'

And he remained infuriated that he'd been suspended for more than two years before he was finally charged. But Ross's stiff upper lip remained firmly in place. Despite all his anger, he insisted he still believed in the Scottish justice system and said he aimed to win his appeal and be proved innocent.

One hundred and fifty miles south, at the Black Watch base at Fort George near Inverness, Michael Ross by now had his own partner and two young daughters and the family lived in army accommodation. He had naturally been advised to keep away from the media scrum that followed Eddy's release from prison. His parents and family back in St Olaurged him to try and get on with his life and forget about Kirkwall and all those 'problems.'

But that would be a lot easier said than done.

# 23.

EDDY ROSS'S TRANSFORMATION from recently released prison inmate into a pillar of society was almost seamless. As one fellow resident said, 'Within weeks of him getting out of prison, people here seemed to have completely forgotten he'd just served time.'

To Ross, this was further evidence of his own innocence, as well as that of his son, who was now proving himself a selfless hero for the nation with the Black Watch regiment. One British Legion member later recalled, 'Eddy looked happy as Larry back at the clubhouse chatting to all the members. There was even a close-knit group of his friends who'd often go into a huddle in the far corner of the bar to discuss their opinions on everything from impending wars in the Middle East to the proposed disbandment of some British regiments, including the Black Watch.'

A member of the club where Eddy so often held court said, 'Eddy was greeted like a long-lost war hero returning from the front. That's how it felt. I don't know for sure but I wouldn't be surprised if he got a round of applause when he first walked back into that clubhouse after getting out of prison.'

But it wasn't all a bed of roses for Ross at the Legion. A small group of members didn't believe he or Michael were innocent and they refused to go to the clubhouse after his release from prison. Many years later, one of them said, 'There was Eddy at the Legion clubhouse, bold as brass, and we all believed Michael was guilty of murdering that poor fella. But Eddy would have nothing of it. He always thought he was right, even when it came to his son's role in a murder. But instead of voicing our disgust we simply boycotted the clubhouse, which was pretty pathetic when I look back on it. And there were only a handful of us anyway, so what did it really matter if we weren't there? In my case it was down to my missus. She said that if we ever went to the clubhouse we were effectively giving Michael permission to have murdered an innocent man.'

But as with so many other aspects of the Mahmood murder and the Ross family's alleged involvement, no one had the courage to confront Ross to his face. The same source said, 'To be honest about it, we all found Eddy a bit of a scary character. My wife forbade me from confronting him because she genuinely feared that either he or Michael might come after us.'

In Inverness, detectives listened to reports from their colleagues in Kirkwall about the return of Ross with astonishment. One now-retired officer said, 'Eddy Ross was back and he didn't seem to have a care in the world. Michael was away with the army, so he was out of the way. Things were looking up for the Ross family. And we still had an unsolved murder on our hands, even though most of us knew who the killer was.'

Five years had now elapsed since the murder of Shamsuddin Mahmood. Other murder enquiries had come and gone for the Inverness-based detectives. Yet the magnitude of the Kirkwall killing exceeded all. As one former officer said, 'If anything we had worked doubly hard to try and prosecute Michael because of Eddy Ross being a copper. His arrogance at the time of the original investigation had infuriated many of us and we remained determined to make sure Michael did not get away with murder. But Eddy's imprisonment completely watered down our efforts to a certain degree and now so much time had elapsed that the killing of Shamsuddin Mahmood itwas on the verge of being classified as a cold case in investigative terms. That meant it would be most likely be put in a drawer and forgotten about.' The files on the murder in a cold case were put to one side until a significant piece of new evidence emerged that would lead to a prosecution.

Ross insisted to friends and associates that Michael would never be prosecuted because he didn't do it. Detectives were once again feeling increasingly frustrated because it felt as if he was rubbing their noses in it yet again. Despite Ross's prosecution and subsequent incarceration the family's so-called supporters had already made up their minds that Michael Ross had done nothing wrong. One of them still said, many years later, 'Michael did not commit that murder and it was about time the police in Inverness admitted they were wrong to point the finger at him and Eddy.'

Naturally, Eddy Ross and his 'people' wouldn't let the matter go. One Kirkwall resident said, 'We all thought that Eddy's imprisonment would mark a watershed moment in the case. OK, the police hadn't got the killer but they'd managed the next best thing by prosecuting Eddy. After he'd gone off to prison, the community seemed relieved and the memories of that murder began to fade for the first time since the killing itself. Then two years later Eddy is back on the streets of Kirkwall rallying his "troops" down at the British Legion and acting as if he had done nothing wrong in the first place.'

Ross cannily avoided talking publicly about the case at this time but happily sat back and allowed others to voice not only their opinions about the murder, but also about the innocence of himself and his son. One former fellow citizen said, 'One morning around that time, I heard two old boys in a café in Kirkwall discussing the case in the most shocking terms. They didn't seem to care whether Eddy and Michael were involved in the murder, they were more concerned with tainting the victim.

'They kept saying, What does it matter? It was some Indian and he probably got what he deserved for being mixed up in drugs and crime. Eddy's boy did us all a favour when he killed him. Now he's with the Black Watch serving his country. Good luck to him.'"

Eddy Ross was now receiving just fifty-one pounds a week in Jobseeker's Allowance with two years to go on parole following his release from prison. When a job at a local undertaker was offered to him he snapped it up, although there were some in Kirkwall who found this particular new career change ironic considering what his son was suspected of doing.

In the middle of all this, Michael Ross quietly returned to Kirkwall for a few days and married his local childhood sweetheart. His other half was by all accounts an extremely shy woman and her identity was fiercely protected by the Ross family. They genuinely feared that someone might come after Michael and his new bride because of what they called those 'wild accusations' linking him to the Mahmood murder. Michael later admitted explaining to his wife about being accused of murder but he never said publicly if he had told her he was guilty or innocent. Inside the Black Watch regiment, he was already using his experience with guns to becomea firearms instructor with the regiment.

During one of Michael's brief visits to Kirkwall, Eddy persuaded him to go to the British Legion clubhouse in the centre of town for a pint and a chat with members. One of them later said, 'Michael was a real hero to many of us old vets down at the Legion. We all swarmed around him listening to his stories about the Black Watch while Eddy looked on proudly.'

Michael must have sensed there were vastly polarised opinions about him in Kirkwall, although he tried to put on a brave face in front of his father and those Legion vets. One of his oldest friends in Kirkwall later said, 'Michael seemed even more detached after he joined the army. I bumped into him once in Kirkwall and he told me he no longer considered Kirkwall to be home and it was a relief to him. I know he married and settled down but I could tell that something – presumably the murder – still hung over him, even though he tried to give the impression it wasn't important. But I knew the real Michael from back when that poor Bangladeshi guy was murdered. Michael often made racist comments that didn't really bother any of us because a lot of kids back then said stuff like that.

Often it was down to plain ignorance that came through their fathers who were stuck in the past. But the trouble was back then there was no one telling kids like Michael to wise up and stop being filled with hate and prejudice. It wasn't just about race, either. He seemed homophobic and he even hated anyone he ever suspected of taking drugs.'

Not far from where Michael Ross lived near Inverness with his wife and two children, the detectives who'd failed to mount a murder prosecution against him were infuriated every time they picked up a newspaper and saw how many in Kirkwall refused to accept that Michael Ross might be the actual killer of Mahmood.

In 2000, after months of closure due to a downturn in business, and several failed attempts to sell up, the Mumtaz restaurant was sold to a new owner. Iqbal Choudhury immediately re-opened the restaurant under a new name, Eastern Spice. The time had come to put the Mumtaz, and all that its name connoted, to bed, once and for all.

# 24.

MICHAEL ROSS'S SUPERIOR officers at the Black Watch regiment considered him to be an exceptional soldier in the making. His target practice results were way above average and he was supremely confident handling any type of weapon, even those large, heavy rifles used for long-distance targets.

It was not surprising that Ross's ability as a marksman eventually helped earmark him for a specialised role inside the Black Watch regiment's exclusive sniper unit. Eddy Ross was delighted when he heard about Michael's elevation. He'd always had the utmost respect for snipers when he'd served with the regiment back in Northern Ireland and now his son's regiment was about to be posted to the killing fields of Iraq in the aftermath of 9/11.

When the British army was contacted by local and national newspapers about the rumours still surrounding Ross a spokesperson said, 'Michael Ross is innocent until proven guilty. The case in question had no bearing on him joining the army. He is a good soldier serving his country with distinction.' As if to prove their loyalty to Ross, the army then elevated him to the rank of lance corporal with the Black Watch.

He was about to depart for Basra, Iraq, when his second daughter was born at the services' accommodation that was the family home near Inverness. Ross seemed to have turned his life around admirably.

Elsewhere in Inverness, Detective Inspector Angus Chisholm was retiring from the police force. No doubt he was frustrated not to have brought Michael Ross to justice. Chisholm then took a new post as office manager for the procurator fiscal, Andrew Laing.

Behind the scenes, senior Northern Constabulary officers seemed to have accepted that unless they could uncover some new evidence, Michael Ross would never be brought to justice. His father continued to vent his anger about any comments made by the mainland police in relation to the case. He was especially infuriated when one senior police officer told a newspaper that the Mahmood murder was 'definitely' racially motivated. Ross must have feared that such emotive terms would put pressure on the police to re-open the case and try once again to bring the killer to justice.

Nursing an overwhelming sense of injustice and a belief in his family's innocence, Eddy Ross couldn't resist speaking out publicly and told one reporter during a meeting at a Kirkwall hotel, 'Look, I was convicted for a crime I did not commit. That's it. But unless you want to give me a million pounds to take them on, what can I do? What did I do? I don't know what I did other than telling them about this ammunition.' He also insisted he was no longer angry about his prosecution, although few believed him. 'I was angry then. It's passed now.

People can make up their own minds. I'm fifty-three and I'm on the downward slope like everyone else. I get on with my life. Just understand this. I did nothing wrong.'

Ross even claimed that he still sometimes wondered about his own son's innocence. 'But where is the proof? Why has Michael Ross not been charged with murder? I was looking at him as my son, but also the son of a policeman, and I genuinely never had an inclination either physically or emotionally to indicate he did it. Maybe I'm blind. I used to look at him and think to myself, If he did it he is either a psychopath or the coolest hit man in the world. If he did it he should be working for the mafia.'

But Eddy steadfastly refused to allow journalists to speak directly to his son. 'Because I know how the press twist things. So I've told him not to speak to them. He's got his own life to lead now. But he's got nothing to hide.' So who killed Shamsuddin Mahmood? And, why? Ross was asked the key questions by one reporter. He sighed, studiously absorbed in how he could answer this question. 'In all honesty,' Ross eventually said, 'I don't want to talk or speculate about anything outside the sphere of my own family. I've got my wife and three kids to think about.' Besides Michael, Eddy Ross had a seventeen-year-old daughter and his younger son, Colin, had recently joined a commando unit of the Royal Marines. 'The pressure on the family has been pretty immense,' Eddy conceded to a journalist. Then, referring back to the question of who killed Mahmood, he added, 'Quite honestly, I haven't really thought about that aspect.'

The case, once described as a 'thousand-piece jigsaw', seemed destined to remain unsolved.

* * *

# THE SNIPER'S STORY

Being a sniper is different from any other role in wartime. And snipers need immense patience and a chilling indifference towards their intended target. 'It's all about watching and then killing, in that order,' one retired US Army marksman recently said.

As US and its allies surged through Iraq in 2003, snipers like Michael Ross were the lifeblood for many of their colleagues. They were the eyes and ears who ensured the regiment's survival out in the field. This must have often involved Michael Ross watching crowds of locals through gun scope for hours on end, to see if anyone looked suspicious. There might be a child with a grenade or a woman hiding a semi-automatic under her niqab. Threats came from all directions.

Michael had been told during sniper training that there were no obvious targets. Each potential threat had to be sized up and analysed individually in a matter of minutes, sometimes even seconds, before the trigger could be squeezed. Michael Ross and other snipers like him literally had the life of others in his hands. And there was no going back once he pulled that trigger, either. No one knows when he got his first kill in Iraq but from what people said about his character it's unlikely he ever gave it much thought. His father had trained him to be the ultimate, detached soldier, able to switch his emotions on and off in a nanosecond. But then, if detectives were correct, Michael Ross had already tasted his first kill in the unlikeliest of locations: an Indian restaurant in one of the Britain's most isolated communities.

Out on the battlefields of Iraq it was a lot more crowded and that would surely mean Ross's previous 'experience' would count for nothing? Not true, said an expert. 'If Michael did kill Shamsuddin Mahmood then you can safely say that by the time he got to Iraq with the Black Watch, he'd long since learned what it felt like to kill and that is the thing professional soldiers always say. If you've done it once, you'll be able to do it again.'

In fact, the cities and towns of Iraq weren't that different from Kirkwall, with their narrow streets and darkened alleyways. Michael Ross had done enough ducking and diving around his home town to know how to judge any distance in such environments. Many snipers say that just before they pull the trigger they worry what might happen if they've shot an innocent person. Not Michael Ross. He was a professional soldier, an expert in his field. The target was no different from the cut-out man he'd shot at for practice since he was a teenager.

In any case, Ross would not have had time to debate the rights and wrongs of his mission. In the Iraqi insurgent strongholds, every local was a potential enemy. As one ex-sniper later put it, 'The only question to ask yourself is me or them? That usually spurs you on to squeeze the trigger.'

After all, pulling that trigger was all that matters. 'If you hesitated then you or your colleagues might die. It's as simple as that,' said one soldier.

No official figures were available as to how many 'kill missions' Michael Ross carried out in Iraq. Unlike the US authorities, the UK government doesn't sanction going public with such sensitive information. One US soldier in Iraq claimed the most kills in US military history recently. He'd officially shot dead 160 human beings from long range but the soldier himself reckoned the real figure was more like at least 250.

Michael Ross's youthful fondness for so-called thrash metal

music and in particular the sounds of Megadeth would have no doubt resonated with many of his fellow troops in Iraq. Music had evolved over centuries as being an important motivating force when soldiers went into battle, starting with the Black Watch's iconic pipes and drums. Listening to Megadeth on an iPod was common by the time the second Iraq war was under way. No doubt Ross would have been strangely reassured to find that his own taste in music was liked by so many colleagues in both the UK and US forces. Those iPods enabled Michael Ross and many of his fellow troops to 'tune out', with Megadeth providing a constant soundtrack to his experiences in Iraq. Many believe that the increased use of music during the Iraq conflict helped to cut boredom. But there is also evidence that there were much more deep-seated reasons that music like metal dominated the lives of so many troops on the ground. Army units became more unified through a theme of brotherhood, something that superior officers tried to encourage to a certain extent.

As one Iraq war veteran later explained: 'You can zone out with the right type of music, especially when you're in an armoured car or if you're a sniper and you're sitting there for hours waiting for a target to appear.' However, there was a negative side to all this: some experts believed that listening to intense music like death metal could 'pump up' a soldier so much he would lose perspective on his mission. Many troops from US and UK units often hooked their players to sophisticated Bose speaker systems when they were out on patrol in their armoured vehicles. One soldier said, 'The heavier the music the better. If we were going into scary situations then death metal kinda helped us focus, if that makes sense?'

Army snipers don't tend to talk much about their experiences because of the obvious implications of their work. But we know that Ross was often tasked with protecting specific Black Watch units as they tried to keep the peace in Iraq. Most snipers were often used more as a deterrent than actually being the killing machines they were so often portrayed as in the media. Ross would frequently be positioned on rooftops watching through his rifle scope for any hint of an insurgent, as he represented the first line of defence against the militants trying to kill his comrades.

Naturally, army snipers each had their own preferred weapon of choice. The most popular was the British-made sniper rifle L115A3, which could take out a target from up to a mile away. Snipers such as Michael Ross also acted as lookouts, watching everyone and everything coming in and out of a unit compound, as well as sending regular intelligence reports to senior command. They were taught to create profiles on every person of interest they saw on a daily basis. One US sniper said, 'We are the ones with eyes on the ground. It is the logging and reporting of every little detail: the direction he's walked, how far he's walked, what he's wearing, what is he doing, what is he carrying.'

Ross's father Eddy later insisted to this author that being a sniper was only one aspect of Michael's career within the Black Watch. 'There's too much focus on the sniper side of his career. Michael got involved in many other areas of the army which had nothing to do with such things.' Ross must have known what many in Kirkwall were saying: that his son Michael 'learned' how to kill on the innocent streets of Kirkwall and that had now helped turn him into a professional sniper on the far less innocent streets of Iraq.

Eddy Ross was pushing forward with a carefully planned surge of his own; to launch an appeal against his conviction. He even let it be known in Kirkwall that he'd been informed by a police mole that one unnamed, key witness had changed his mind three times about giving evidence in case against him. Eddy Ross told one reporter, 'I cannot get a retrial but, if I can, if I do get something out of what has been said recently and bring my case up in front of the judges and they re-examine what's been said, then obviously I would like my conviction quashed.' Eddy Ross furnished his solicitors with this extra information but admitted to one journalist, 'If nothing comes out of it, I intend to take my own course of action to clear things up.' Some in Kirkwall dreaded to think what 'my own course of action' meant.

Eddy Ross also reiterated to reporters that he had no idea who'd carried out the murder. If had, he said, 'that would be withholding information'. As usual, he steadfastly maintained that his son could not have had anything to do with the murder but fewer and fewer people on the Orkneys believed him. 'From my knowledge,' he said, 'what I saw at the time, what I have read while I was still working, it was not the work of a fifteen-year-old boy, no matter whose son it is.'

That fifteen-year-old schoolboy was now a twenty-five-year-old soldier fighting in one of the world's most deadly trouble spots.

# 25.

ON A BLISTERING hot summer's day in 2004, Michael Ross found himself in a Black Watch armoured vehicle winding its way through a hostile town south of Baghdad. The unit were in a convoy from their FOB (forward operating base) where they'd been staying before driving up to one of their advance units of troops out in the field.

It was a tense journey. Michael and his comrades had been trained to remain super-alert to everything going on around them and multiple threats had been made by insurgents about the British being prime targets. With the armoured vehicle travelling at speed to avoid snipers, there would have been a disconnect between the soldiers and their surroundings. As a result, none of them noticed men watching them avidly from passing rooftops until the vehicle was blown apart by an IED (improvised explosive device), which detonated on the commander's side between the dismount door and the rear tyre. The concussion of the blast blew off the windows and rattled through the truck, causing all of the doors to blow open. It even bent the buckle of each soldier's seatbelt, which then unlatched. Ross was ejected onto the road and slid along for about thirty metres. He must have been completely stunned for a few moments.

Years later, he told his father that the adrenaline then kicked in so strongly he and his fellow soldiers could barely feel whether or not they were injured.

One soldier who went through a similar blast said, 'All you really want to do at that moment is kill the motherfucker who tried to kill you.'

Ross knew he had to keep low, as low as when he'd allegedly dashed down that darkened alleyway in Kirkwall in the early summer of 1994 after Shamsuddin Mahmood had been shot dead. He galloped back to the vehicle to see if his colleagues were OK and noticed Iraqis working in a nearby wheat field as if nothing had happened. Where were the insurgents who'd planted that IED? Were they about to ambush him and his unit from any of the rundown buildings overshadowing the dusty roadway?

As a sniper, Michael Ross knew only too well that someone could easily pick him off from a nearby rooftop. Having got back to his twisted and buckled vehicle, Ross sought out his injured colleagues. The soldier who'd been alongside him in the armoured car just a few moments earlier was lying in a corner of the inside of the vehicle. Ross bent down and started to lift him into a more comfortable position. As Eddy Ross explained to this author many years later: 'Michael said that as he was lifting the man, he noticed he seemed very light. It was only then he realised that the bottom half of his entire body had been completely blown away.'

His commanding officer later described how Ross then assumed control, administering first-aid to his comrades and their Iraqi interpreter and then helping to organise the evacuation of the wounded. He also sat and talked to the soldiers to keep their spirits up while they awaited emergency services. No doubt, as the adrenaline started to wear off, Ross would have become more aware of the seriousness of the situation. But those who knew him back in Kirkwall say they find it hard to imagine Ross crying at any stage. One of them said, 'The Michael I know would have shrugged his shoulders and started looking around for a terrorist to shoot.'

It's not known if Ross suffered any physical injuries during the blast because neither he nor his father will talk about that aspect of his experience – 'but you can be sure that Eddy's training of Michael would have kicked in,' explained a former police colleague. 'That meant staying calm and detached and making sure that he and his fellow soldiers got back to base safely. He was always very matter-of-fact, even from the age of eleven or twelve.'

Back at barracks, Michael reported to his commanding officer to let him know he was all right. Many other soldiers caught in similar incidents have talked afterwards about 're-thinking' their intentions to stay in the army. One said, 'I think a big part of it was, and still is, that there are so many people trying to destroy our lives, and our country's way of life, that we need as many people as possible to kill them before they get the chance.'

No one knows what was going on inside Ross's head that day but one of his old friends in Kirkwall said, 'Michael would have bottled it all up I guess. But maybe that's not such a bad thing because it meant Michael was never ripped to shreds emotionally speaking by things like this. That makes him a more professional soldier in my book.'

No doubt Ross was given a lot of support by his commanding officer and sergeant major, as well as the entire troop. And then there was his family waiting for him in Scotland. It wouldn't have been easy for them to hear what had happened. Ross insisted to his friends and family on visits back to the Scottish mainland and the Orkneys that he was 'just doing my job'. He saw his actions as being part of a team effort and it was clear that his loyalty to his comrades was unquestionable.

Back in the early 1990s, when Eddy Ross toughened up his son with those gruelling training exercises across the heathland overlooking Scapa Flow, he no doubt continually lectured Michael about the importance of loyalty. That loyalty had been tested to the limit in the aftermath of the murder of Shamsuddin Mahmood and now Ross's loyalty had kicked in on the murderous streets of Iraq.

Ross clearly always managed to focus on the task at hand. He never seemed fazed, even when bombs were going off all around him, not to mention bullets streaking past him from all directions. One colleague said that Ross was always one of the first soldiers to tend to his colleague's wounds whenever they were under heavy fire. 'Michael sometimes behaved as if he had a death wish. He seemed incapable of feeling fear but it made him one hell of a soldier.' In Iraq, firefight must have helped keep Ross well away from dealing with that other battlefront – back in Kirkwall.

Towards the end of 2004, Michael Ross and his Black Watch comrades were ordered by the government led by Tony Blair to help US forces throw a 'ring of steel' around the embattled

Iraqi city of Fallujah in preparation for an all-out assault on insurgents. This meant the Black Watch coming under the command of US marines at Camp Dogwood in Iraq. The 850-strong 1st Battalion of the Black Watch – including three companies of armoured infantry, totalling more than five hundred men – were to fight alongside D Squadron of the SAS. The Black Watch soldiers were equipped with fifty Warrior armoured troop carriers and ordered to hold an approach road into Fallujah, where extremists – including notorious terror chief Abu Musab al-Zarqawi – were thought to have their strongholds.

The build-up to the battle of Fallujah tested the mettle of all the troops involved. Checkpoints had to be established around the city to prevent anyone from entering and to intercept insurgents attempting to flee. Overhead, high-tech imagery had been obtained of the terrain to provide micro-detailed maps of the city to be used by allied troops, including the Black Watch regiment. Units were augmented by Iraqi interpreters to assist them with the planned battles. There had already been weeks of air strikes and artillery bombardment to 'soften up' the militants in the city in the hope it would make them more vulnerable to direct attack. And in the middle of all this was twenty-six-year-old Michael Ross, just promoted to sergeant for his bravery during earlier IED attacks. His fellow soldiers were already impressed by Ross's maturity and ability to react calmly under fire and his superior officers felt equally confident in his abilities.

This battle of Fallujah – codenamed Operation Al-Fajr (Arabic for 'the dawn') and Operation Phantom Fury – was expected to last until just before Christmas and would clear the city of all insurgents. On the night of 7 November, US

Navy Seals and Marine reconnaissance snipers and their allied snipers – who may well have included Ross – provided intelligence and target-marking on the city perimeter as ground operations got under way. Attacking from the west and south, the mass of US, Iraqi and allied soldiers soon captured Fallujah general hospital and other important strategic outposts including villages on the Euphrates River along Fallujah's western edge. US troops fired 81mm mortars that thudded into their targets before the troops surged towards the western approaches to the city and secured the Jurf Kas Sukr Bridge.

Nearby, Ross and his unit kept close watch on any possible incursions that might endanger their colleagues. Black Watch snipers were augmented by three seven-man US Navy Seal sniper teams as well as one platoon that provided further advance reconnaissance in the city. The soldiers then used armoured bulldozers to plow the streets and to remain safe and protected from enemy fire.

By 13 November, most of the fighting had subsided, leaving snipers and special forces to wipe out isolated cells of resistance from the insurgents. Coalition forces suffered a total of 107 killed and 613 wounded during Operation Phantom Fury. Iraqi forces lost eight troops with forty-three wounded. Most estimates placed the number of insurgents killed at around 1,200 to 1,500, with some estimations suggesting more than two thousand killed. Coalition forces also captured approximately 1,500 insurgents during the operation.

Ross's commanding officer Lieutenant Colonel Cowan later said that when the regiment was posted at Dogwood, the Black Watch was 'at the limits of a single battalion's capabilities . . . the whole experience was a testing one and all the ranks of the

Black Watch drew together in adversity and came through the stronger for it. The deployment had a certain surreal quality. As a regiment that had never sought the limelight, the Black Watch emerged blinking into the glare of public scrutiny.' Ross was among twelve Black Watch men and women mentioned in dispatches and decorated for their outstanding service during those clashes in Fallujah as well as for their experience in IED attacks in and around Basra.

While Michael Ross was risking life and limb with the Black Watch as they mounted the British army's largest mission in Iraq, defence chiefs in Whitehall were trying to fend off politicians' plans to scrap the entire regiment. There was a vociferous campaign mounted to save the Black Watch and other historic Scottish regiments from amalgamation. The army had plans for a single 'super-regiment' to cover the whole of Scotland as a result of the Labour government's decision to cut the number of infantry battalions from forty to thirty-six. At the British Legion clubhouse in Kirkwall, Eddy Ross and many of his fellow veterans were appalled. Not only was his brave son fighting for his country in a strange and inhospitable land but now politicians were moving ahead with plans to destroy one of the mainstays of the British army, their beloved Black Watch regiment.

As commander-in-chief, the Queen had a constitutional right to be consulted over such changes. She was particularly concerned about the Black Watch because of the Queen Mother's attachment to the regiment; her brother had been serving in it when he was killed in the World War I. Eventually, under a carefully negotiated compromise, the Black Watch was allowed to keep its name – but only as a battalion of a single Scottish regiment.

The publicity about the plans for the Black Watch received wide coverage in the Orkneys and fuelled the opinion of many that Michael Ross – whatever he did as a schoolboy – should be granted 'immunity' because of his status as a war hero. His commanding officer Captain Alexander Ramsay, thirty-one, later described Michael Ross as 'one of the finest soldiers' he had ever known.

One Kirkwall resident later said, 'By this time the majority of islanders knew that in all likelihood Michael Ross *had* killed Shamsuddin Mahmood. But there was a feeling from some that his slate should be wiped clean because he had more than repaid his debt to society through his bravery as a soldier.' In Inverness, detectives ignored all calls for immunity and kept their eyes and ears peeled for any information that might enable them to re-open the cold case and bring the killer to justice.

\* \* \*

Around this time, Michael Ross, his wife and two daughters moved to a barracks in Northern Ireland following some months working as an instructor at the Catterick barracks in Yorkshire. Over ten years in the British army, Michael Ross had served in Bosnia, Iraq and Kosovo. Those battlefields must have felt like another world to him, an environment in which survival or death were the only objectives, places where the past would be put in a box and never mentioned. Now-peaceful Northern Ireland couldn't have been much to his liking because he was only a short hop across the sea from the place where the events of that deadly evening of 2 June 1994 had occurred. Sure, the army offered a certain amount of 'protection' but ultimately Michael Ross must have feared that one day the long arm of the law could still reach out and grab him.

Meanwhile, in comparatively sleepy Kirkwall, Eddy Ross made it clear he was immensely proud of his son. Many of the Ross family supporters in and around the town no doubt felt that the less said about the murder of Shamsuddin Mahmood the better. It had been more than ten years now. Everything seemed to have virtually returned to normal in Kirkwall. But the disturbing spectre of racism was still simmering on the surface of this isolated, old fashioned community.

One Kirkwall resident said, 'There was this group of people who refused to accept that Michael Ross should be brought to justice and they were getting louder and louder in their support of Michael and Eddy. The rest of us tried to avoid confrontations with them but they often seemed to be spoiling for a fight.'

Ironically, some of these so-called 'supporters' blatantly talked in racist jargon that must have infuriated Ross because they were acknowledging that his son was a killer by insisting it didn't matter because his victim was black. Ross didn't want to hear anyone say Michael was a murderer. He insisted that both he and his son was completely innocent.

Eddy still had a few 'friends' at Kirkwall Police station and around this time they started telling him that detectives in Inverness had made it clear they had not yet given up the hunt for the killer of Mahmood after all, despite it now being referred to as a cold case. Some Kirkwall officers were being stopped in the town centre by people who clearly supported the Ross family and they were told to 'drop it'. This may have been extremely counter-productive for Ross and his son. Some officers felt they were being bullied by supporters of one of their former colleagues. It felt like a deliberate attempt to interfere with the wheels of justice and some at the police station decided to step up their enquiries in the face of such intimidation.

Down in Inverness, retired detective Angus Chisholm's job as office manager to Inverness prosecutor Andrew Laing enabled him to speak in great detail about the case to his boss. The prosecutor assured Chisholm that if his former police colleagues could come up with something new then he would still consider prosecuting Michael Ross. Chisholm passed this information on to detectives in Inverness and, in the middle of 2006, investigators visited Kirkwall to try and reassure the local police that they were still actively hunting for the killer of Mahmood.

In Kirkwall, two detectives from Inverness also pointed out to the local police that their number one suspect had moved out of the community. This, inferred investigators, meant that their suspect could not threaten or intimidate any vital witnesses who had previously failed to come forward, at the time of the killing. One former officer said, 'What the officers from Inverness said made complete sense. Their suspect Michael Ross had scared the shit out of most people when he lived here before and after the murder. But now he was living and working elsewhere.' The Inverness detectives urged Kirkwall police to go back to their files and seek out anyone who might have been reluctant to help back at the time of the killing. 'Ten years had gone by. There was no reason to hide any more. This was the perfect moment to try and find the missing pieces to the jigsaw.'

However, there were a small minority of police officers in Kirkwall who didn't want to hear the name Michael Ross ever again. The murder had been a dark chapter in the history of the Orkneys and they wanted it to be left alone so the islands could move on in peace. The guilt or innocence of Ross wasn't relevant to them any more. Eventually, one police officer at Kirkwall station with no connections whatsoever to Eddy Ross was assigned the task of re-interviewing and tracking down anyone who'd refused to help back at the time of the murder. It meant knocking on a lot of doors – some of which were slammed in his face – but he soldiered on. One retired officer said, 'The detectives from Inverness put us under quite a lot of pressure. They clearly believed we could get a breakthrough if we were determined enough. A lot of us just sighed. We didn't think we stood a chance of nailing Michael Ross for the killing, despite Eddy's conviction and imprisonment. It was a difficult time to say the least. Most of us just wanted to get on with our day-to-day duties. Sure we all knew who the chief suspect was but by this time most of us had accepted that it would be impossible to bring him to justice.

'It was all very well for the Inverness detectives to accuse us of a cover-up but they didn't have to live in this small community where everyone overlapped with everyone else. In any case, Eddy Ross was still making it clear he would fight tooth-and-nail to stop Michael being arrested. A few of my colleagues still questioned Michael's guilt. He was a war hero. What was the point in pulling him in? He wasn't a danger to anyone else. As a result, there was this feeling almost of panic at Kirkwall police station. Some just didn't want to face up to the truth of the situation, which was that we were all responsible for allowing a cold-blooded killer to get away with murder.'

## THE SNIPER'S STORY

Yet again, the murder of Shamsuddin Mahmood was ripping apart the community, all those years after it had happened.

# 26.

ON 2 SEPTEMBER 2006 a middle-aged man walked into Kirkwall police station with what he called an 'anonymous note' and handed it to police clerical worker Susan Sinclair, twenty-seven, who was on the desk at the police station at the time.

Susan Sinclair immediately recognised the man as local labourer William 'Willy' Grant. Miss Sinclair later said, 'I opened the letter and read it and passed it on to DC Petrie.'

Grant's 'anonymous' letter read:

> *This is a true letter, I promise that I saw the person who killed the Indian waiter. I saw his face in full and the handgun. It was in toilets at Kiln Corner.*
>
> *The person was about fifteen-plus years approx., white and had a balaclava on head but still not turned down.*
>
> *The colour was either dark blue or black and dark*

> *clothing. He came out of the cubicle but went back in*
> *quick when he saw me.*
>
> *I looked over and saw his face in full. The handgun*
> *was natural polished metal or silver and a big Beretta.*
>
> *This may seem stupid but the way he held the*
> *handgun looked like he had held a firearm before. I just*
> *don't ken what to do. Worried sick witness.*

It was plainly obvious the writer was Willy Grant himself. He'd even been approached by police a few days earlier when they were looking for new information about the killing but had said nothing. His name had originally cropped up during the initial investigation because he'd claimed to have seen Michael Ross in Kirkwall in the local toilets at the time of the murder. But back in 1994, Grant's claims had been dismissed by officers because he was considered an unreliable witness due to the vagueness of his claims. However, Grant was now insisting in his 'anonymous' letter that he'd clearly seen Michael Ross on the evening of the murder wearing a balaclava and handling a gun in the toilets near the crime scene. Kirkwall police immediately re-interviewed Willy Grant and announced that they were now taking his evidence very seriously.

Grant also told officers that he'd witnessed Ross shouting racial abuse outside the restaurant a couple of days before the murder. Grant later said he'd only come forward twelve years after Mahmood's death, because he was now afraid of 'certain people' on the Orkneys. Eddy Ross later described Grant's evidence as 'laughable', saying, 'A man hands in an anonymous letter he himself wrote. It's complete joke.'

Over in Northern Ireland, with the Black Watch regiment,

Michael Ross was fed news about the rebooted investigation by his father and what he heard convinced him he was the subject of a 'witch-hunt'. He later said, 'Over the years, the Mumtaz murder would be in the news from time to time and very often I would be mentioned in relation to it. This felt like a form of harassment to me and my family.'

Of course, Ross was a very different character from the punch-happy, cold-blooded teenager he'd once appeared to be. No doubt his experiences in Iraq and elsewhere had had a profound effect on him, although many in his regiment said he never showed any signs of stress and remained immensely calm under pressure. But then he had been taught not to express his feelings because that was a sign of weakness in the eyes of many old-fashioned soldiers.

Eddy and Moira Ross were no doubt relieved that their son remained well away from Kirkwall in 2006. But it was starting to dawn on them that the police enquiry had been re-invigorated by Willy Grant's anonymous letter, which they were now taking very seriously. Michael Ross's Black Watch officers were then informed of stories in the media that mentioned he was under investigation once again as a murder suspect. Ross himself later said, 'The army asked me if I wanted a lawyer. I said, "No," because I knew it would be more rubbish.'

And in the middle of all this, some in his 'camp' of supporters came up with a new, more eloquent reason for questioning the wisdom in re-investigating the case. It was pointed out that chief suspect Michael Ross had been an adolescent child when he was alleged to have committed the killing. Now he was a Black Watch sergeant who'd seen active service in Iraq. 'In other words, how could this man be held responsible for something he might have done when he was a child?' said one Kirkwall resident. Others pointed out that if Ross was prosecuted and found guilty twelve years earlier, he would – as a child – have faced a maximum sentence of about six or seven years, which would mean he'd by now be a free man.

Eddy Ross must have been infuriated by such comments because he knew only too well that his son would never have become a war hero if he'd been imprisoned back then. He would not have been accepted into the Black Watch regiment as a convicted killer. Others still were insisting that the case against Michael should be dropped because the procurator fiscal had seen all the evidence back in 1995 and decided there was not enough to pursue a case against him. The only completely fresh piece of evidence appeared to be in that letter – laughingly described as anonymous – from a highly questionable source. There remained no scientific evidence linking Michael Ross to the crime.

Inverness detectives reappeared in Kirkwall soon after the letter was handed in and decided Willy Grant could now be crucial to their decision to push for Michael Ross to finally be prosecuted for the murder of Shamsuddin Mahmood. After all, the writer of that letter had seen Michael on the evening of the murder wearing a balaclava and holding a gun. In interview with detectives, Willy Grant insisted he didn't know Michael or his family personally because he was living on one of the islands at the time of the murder. However Grant said that his niece, who went to Kirkwall grammar school, had pointed Ross out to him and that was when he got to know the identity of the man he both saw in Kirkwall town centre on the night of the murder and shouting racist abuse a couple of days before that.

Willy Grant's decision to finally come forward after twelve years split the local community down the middle. Some said that Grant's attempt at anonymity was 'pathetic' and summed up a fragile state of mind. Others applauded him for having the courage to finally help investigators solve the most notorious crime ever committed on the Orkneys. Within days of delivering that letter to the police, father of four Willy Grant found himself receiving threats from those 'certain people'. He later said, 'The first was from a lad in his twenties in a pub. As he walked by, he said, "By the way, there's a price on your head." It was sheer fear . . . terror. Thankfully I was sitting down as my legs turned to jelly. I went to the toilet and cried.'

Grant claimed he was then assaulted in a local supermarket by a woman he had gone to school with. He said, 'She grabbed me by the arm and called me a few unprintable names. She made it clear it was to do with the court case.' Then came a third incident when, as Grant was walking down a Kirkwall street, a man told him he would be 'the next bastard to be shot'. Grant also later claimed that 'sinister' letters were sent to his new home on the other side of the island, in Stromness. The first letter contained a press cutting and the second letter included a Masonic emblem, along with his name and the name of an officer from the murder inquiry who happened to be a member of the Freemasons.

Grant openly admitted to being a member of the Freemasons himself and being connected to the policeman named in the note. But he strongly denied that freemasonry had anything to do with his decision to give evidence. He said he was stunned by the letter and felt threatened by it.

The clear implication was that Grant had been 'persuaded' by his fellow Freemasons to go to the police to ensure that Michael Ross was brought to justice. Grant believed both letters were from one person because the brand of both envelopes was the same. Also, both were handwritten and it looked as if the writer had used the wrong hand in one to try and disguise it. He told local reporters he deeply regretted writing the letter to the police in the first place. 'I wish now that I'd left it alone,' he said. 'I'm like a prisoner in my home. I don't go out at night. I'm too scared. I feel like I'm on a very thin layer of ice.'

The procurator fiscal, Andrew Laing, told police he was finally prepared to sign off on the arrest warrant for Michael Ross. The decision was kept under wraps from the police in Kirkwall because detectives in Inverness were determined that this time Eddy Ross would not get advance notice of their intentions.

In late September 2006, ten police officers flew to Belfast, drove in convoy to the barracks where Michael Ross was stationed and arrested him on suspicion of murder. One officer who was present at the arrest said, 'Michael looked shell-shocked. He hadn't seen it coming but he agreed to come with us without any fuss.' He was officially charged with murder, disposal of a weapon and clothing, committing a 'breach of the peace' in Papdale Woods and a racist 'breach of the peace' offence that was connected to the incident described by Willy Grant outside the restaurant a couple of days before the murder. Ross's solicitor said his client would be lodging a special alibi defence against the murder charge on the basis that he had witnesses who would say he was not in the vicinity of the restaurant at the time of Mahmood's murder. And Michael Ross was given bail at his first court appearance while lawyers prepared for the case. Eddy Ross was delighted because he interpreted this decision as meaning his son was not considered any threat to anyone, further proof to him of his son's obvious innocence. But to many others, Michael Ross appeared in a complete state of denial. Why couldn't he finally just face up to the consequences of his actions?

# 27.

ON 15 MAY 2008, fourteen long years after the murder was committed, the police's one and only suspect, Michael Ross, now twenty-nine, found himself in the dock in Glasgow crown court. He denied all the charges.

The press area and public gallery were packed, as they would be throughout the trial. The early stages revived deeply disturbing memories for many of those present in the restaurant on the night of the murder. Newspaper stories with gaudy headlines once again reported how 'a young girl was sprayed with blood and gore when a gunman executed a waiter at point-blank range in an Indian restaurant'. This must have further compounded the post-traumatic stress aspects of the attack that had changed so many people's lives for ever. Local businessman Donald Glue, his wife and two children had been giving their order to Mahmood at the very moment he was shot dead and they remained deeply traumatised by the events of 2 June 1994.

## THE SNIPER'S STORY

Mr Glue, now fifty-four, gave eyewitness testimony to the jury in front of a hushed court. He told how the bullet from the shooter destroyed the side of Shamsuddin Mahmood's face and that his own daughter Sarah was covered in what had been his face. Michael Ross sat grim-faced in the dock as Sarah Glue, now twenty-six, broke down in tears as she recalled the same horrifying scene. She said, 'When the gun went off, I wasn't aware of what had happened. It then became obvious.'

The high court in Glasgow heard about the anonymous letter sent by Willie Grant, who told the court he'd seen Michael Ross on the evening of the murder wearing a balaclava and holding a gun. Grant also told the court he'd heard Ross and another boy shouting racial abuse and threatening violence outside the Indian restaurant previously, although this charge against Michael would later be dropped. Another witness at the trial was retired BT engineer John Rendall, seventy-four, who told how he heard banging and rustling coming from a cubicle in the toilets at Kiln Corner, minutes after the waiter was gunned down. He said he then saw a man walking away down the street.

Detective Inspector Iain Smith, Northern Constabulary's senior investigating officer, told the court it was a 'shocking and sickening crime'. He said that Ross had been the force's only main suspect throughout the fourteen-year investigation and 'in all probability' it was a racially motivated crime.

Under cross-examination by Donald Findlay QC for the defence, a woman who attended cadets with Michael Ross and had once dated him admitted that she and all her friends in the cadets, including Ross, used racist terms. She told the court that she would not use words like that now because 'it's wrong'.

Findlay then asked her, 'Did you ever then or now see any sign in Michael Ross that he actually wanted to do harm to Asian people, black people?'

She replied, 'No.'

The court also heard from Eddy Ross's one-time friend, ex-marine James Spence. He revealed how he was asked to lie about the stolen ammunition by Eddy Ross. Retired detective inspector Angus Chisholm told the court that Michael Ross had claimed to police he was cycling at the time of the shooting. Chisholm told the court that all of Ross's 'friends' had denied seeing him on the night Mahmood was shot dead. Tapes from the 1994 police interviews with Michael Ross were then played to the jury.

Chisholm's voice could be clearly heard on the tapes saying, 'You're saying you were sure you were there and they are saying you weren't. Someone is lying.'

Ross replied, 'It's not me. I was definitely there.'

A decision not to let Ross give evidence at his own trial was significant because it seemed to imply he wasn't trustworthy enough. Michael himself had wanted to go in the stand but his barrister had insisted this would be a bad idea. Coverage of his trial was punctuated by photos and footage of him defiantly entering court each morning, having remained on bail throughout the hearing. Some were shocked that a man facing such serious charges was not being kept in custody. Ross supporters insisted that the decision of the court to trust him enough not to flee meant that he must be innocent. Ross seemed confident, almost cocky, as he strolled along the pavement on the way to the court each morning, surrounded by press photographers and cameramen.

One journalist later said, 'He looked as if he had it in the bag. That he would not be going to jail and there was this cold look in his eyes as if to say, "I don't give a fuck about any of you. Now get out of my way or I'll . . . "'

On 13 June, it was Eddy Ross's turn to take the witness stand. He denied covering up his son's alleged involvement in the murder. The court was told how Eddy Ross, now fifty-seven, had been jailed for four years in 1997 for attempting to pervert the course of justice. Ross insisted to Donald Findlay that he only ever had one sealed box of bullets and denied ever receiving an additional, open box from Jim Spence or asking him to lie about it.

Findlay told the court, 'It is obviously the case, if you are telling us the truth today, that you were in 1997 the victim of a miscarriage of justice?'

Ross replied, 'I believe so, sir.'

After completing his evidence, Eddy Ross went to sit up in the public gallery where a bulletproof screen separated him from the main courtroom. He later said it was hard to hear everything being said, so he leaned forward most of the time straining to listen to the proceedings. He heard Findlay insist to the court that Michael Ross was not a hooligan when he was fifteen. Michael had lived in the country, was in the army cadets and target-shooting was his main sport.

Ross's commanding officer and soldiers of different ranks in the Black Watch then informed the court that there was no sign of racism in Michael Ross's behaviour. His comrades stressed in their testimonies that he was a respected and brave NCO who showed compassion to those for whom he had responsibility, regardless of ethnicity. The court heard how Ross had been commended for his part in dealing with the aftermath of those IED attacks. Captain Alexander Ramsay, thirty-one, described Ross as a gentleman and 'one of the finest soldiers, if not the finest soldier, I've commanded'.

But crown prosecutor Brian McConnachie, QC, told the court that, as a youth, Michael Ross had harboured extreme racist views. He had even been heard to say at one time that 'blacks should be shot and have a gun put to their head'. Shortly after this evidence was heard, the court adjourned for the weekend. Less than twenty-four hours later Michael Ross, still out on bail, attended a Black Watch regiment function. A letter sent to police later described when happened when a Black Watch piper approached Michael Ross:

'Did you do it, Michael?'

Ross allegedly replied, 'Of course I did, but they'll never prove it because Dad got rid of all the evidence.'

# 28.

ON 18 JUNE 2008, prosecutor Brian McConnachie, QC, began his closing speech by telling the jury there was a 'compelling circumstantial case' against Michael Ross. He described Ross as a 'cold-blooded assassin' and the murder as 'savage, merciless and pointless'.

McConnachie told the court that the case against Ross was like a jigsaw puzzle. He said to the jury, 'The pieces of evidence demonstrate beyond a shadow of doubt Michael Ross murdered Shamsuddin Mahmood. The big picture is very, very simple. It is a murder committed by a masked gunman. What the evidence does is, piece by piece, remove the mask and, when the mask is removed, we're all staring at Michael Ross.' McConnachie said if the jury believed Ross's alibi – that he was chatting with friends in Kirkwall's Eastabist housing estate when Shamsuddin Mahmood was shot – then he could not have committed the murder. But McConnachie added, 'The three people quite simply do not support his alibi in any way, shape or form.'

McConnachie told the jury the descriptions of Ross at Papdale Woods were strikingly similar to those of the gunman who carried out the shooting. He asked, 'How unlucky can one person be? How unlucky can Michael Ross be that the person who carried out this murder bears such a striking similarity to him? This person commits this murder using 9mm 2Z ammunition. This is the same type of stolen military ammunition that his father, Edmund Ross, got from ex-Marine James Spence. This is a remarkable and extremely unfortunate coincidence for Michael Ross. But luck and coincidence had nothing to do with this. What you have is a completely unanswerable case that Michael Ross, three months before his sixteenth birthday, shot and murdered Shamsuddin Mahmood in the Mumutaz restaurant at 7.15 p.m. on 2 June 1994.'

Donald Findlay QC, defending Michael Ross, accused prosecutors of launching a sustained attack on Ross's character, saying, 'It has been claimed he is racist, sexist and a Nazi.' He said that Ross was not a homicidal maniac but a gentle family man who had served his country in Iraq with distinction. 'I have to prove nothing at all. If I say to you that man did not shoot Mr Mahmood, I don't have to prove who did.' Then defender Findlay insisted to the jury that the shooting had all the hallmarks of a professional hit. 'Witnesses speak of impressions of a hit man. It is as close up and personal as you can get. There are no nerves, anxiety or fear on the part of the shooter. Is that consistent with a fifteen-year-old boy? This is not to do with someone having the ability to pick up a gun, load it and pull the trigger. It is one matter to shoot at a piece of wood with a target on it. It is a very, very different thing to take the life of a human being. Not a single solitary witness suggested that it would occur to them this might be someone in their mid-teens.'

The jury of ten women and five men then retired to consider their verdict and the judge adjourned the case until the following day.

That evening, Michael Ross and his father were convinced he'd be acquitted of all charges. Michael was so confident, he decided to rent a car to take to court the following day so that he could go off on a holiday after the verdict. Well, at least that was the impression Ross gave to the Avis car rental company in Glasgow when he hired a Ford Fiesta. The next morning, Ross left the vehicle in a Tesco car park less than a mile from Glasgow crown court. Then he carefully checked the contents of the boot before walking the rest of the way.

Inside the boot was a cache of arms – including a machine pistol, a rifle, a grenade, knives, camouflage clothing, bullets and binoculars. The grenade was an anti-personnel type that would throw out fragments of metal at high velocity, with the sole purpose of causing death or serious injury. It was lethal up to 30 metres. Ross had smuggled the Scorpion machine pistol back from Kosovo, where he'd served, hidden in a TV set. The grenade had been handed to him after a live firing session at the army base in Catterick where he'd been more recently based. Ross later insisted that after the case ended he'd planned to 'head for the hills and live rough', using the weapons to kill fish and game.

But others are convinced that Ross had decided that if he'd been found guilty he was 'going out with a bang' and would take as many people with him as possible. Whatever the truth of the matter, Ross had carefully planned, as if this was something like another military operation. He'd collected the weapons over a period of time, stored them and then armed them before putting them in the boot of that rented car. To describe the grenade and gun as hunting weapons was completely ludicrous. The machine pistol was later described by an expert as being 'designed to kill numerous people quickly'.

Minutes after parking, Ross strode purposefully up the steps of the court house as he had done each morning over the previous six weeks. Moments later, he was back in the dock awaiting the jury's verdict. He looked down most of the time. But as the hours passed by, his confidence clearly grew and he began studying many of those in the court that day. Ross's legal advisers told him that the longer the jury took, the more likely they were to acquit him.

After deliberating for four hours, the jury announced they were ready to give their verdict. Michael Ross was told by the judge to remain standing. The court went deathly quiet as the jury foreman was asked for a verdict.

'Guilty of murder,' he said.

Michael Ross was also found guilty of attempting to defeat the ends of justice by disposing of the murder weapon and changing his clothing. All verdicts had been by a majority verdict of the jury. Judge Lord Hardie immediately told Ross that he would defer sentence until 11 July for a social-enquiry report, and remanded him in custody. He said, 'You had a distinguished career and served this country well for a period of years, but despite that you committed these shocking crimes.'

For the few moments between the jury's verdict and the judge's comments, Michael Ross looked stunned as the court then fell quiet. But as with so many aspects of his life, Michael Ross had planned meticulously for this day.

# 29.

MICHAEL ROSS GLANCED intensely around the room as the prison officers on either side of him rose to escort him down a handful of steps next to the dock to the cells beneath the court.

Suddenly, Ross knocked the officers out of the way, jumped over the dock, crouching down and dashing towards a fire exit. Ross's QC, Donald Findlay, chased after him, shouting, '*No, Michael! No!*' Findlay later said he blamed himself for not noticing the strain that Ross was under during the murder trial.

As Ross scrambled towards the fire exit, he was rugby-tackled by court official Gordon Morison who pinned him to the ground as Ross tried to hit him. Three other men then kept him on the ground while he was handcuffed before being hauled down the steps to the cells beneath the building. Unknown to everyone present in that court that day, Michael Ross's rental car was parked nearby – packed full of weapons, explosions and bullets.

# THE SNIPER'S STORY

Today, experts say that it was likely that had Ross had got out of the court building, he would have ended up in a firefight with police and that innocent bystanders might well have been hurt or even killed. Some compared Ross's plan to that of US spree killers, determined to take out as many people as possible before either turning the gun on himself or heading into the hills as he later claimed was his intention.

Eddy Ross later shrugged off his son's escape attempt and arsenal of weapons. 'That is a separate issue. Michael was wrong but it had nothing to do with the murder but I can see where he was coming with that. He's a professional soldier, nothing more.'

Back in St Ola, friends and supporters of the Ross family were appalled by the way the trial in Glasgow had panned out and were deeply disturbed by Michael Ross's escape attempt. They all knew it would greatly damage his claims of innocence. These supporters had been utterly convinced Ross was not guilty and many still refused to accept his guilt despite his attempt to flee the court. And Eddy Ross told his family and friends, 'The court case was full of absolute lies and distortions. I know it looks like a good story but nothing connects on this story.' One local businessman who lived just a stone's throw from the Ross home immediately announced in the local newspaper that he was willing to put up a hundred-thousand-pound reward to capture the real killer of Shamsuddin Mahmood.

Shortly after the end of the trial, Mahmood's brother Abul Shafiuddin made an emotional journey to Orkney to see where his younger brother had been killed. He told reporters, 'The family feel happy with the verdict and happy with the performance of the police. Justice has been done. We are grateful to all who worked to bring the accused to trial.' But the sixty-three-year-old lawyer also admitted that he and his family had for many years lost all hope that the murder would ever be solved and he demanded to know why it had taken so long to bring Ross to justice. 'We were convinced long before the trial started that Michael Ross was the person who killed my brother. We have known for many years. We were frustrated and asking, "Why is this taking such a long time? Why is there no progress in the investigation?" It's been an inordinate delay for this to come to trial. We would like it investigated.'

In Kirkwall, the town's Asian community remained very small, just three or four families, and they kept a low profile throughout the trial. Iqbal Ali Choudhury – who now owned the Mumutaz – told local reporters he had never experienced any trouble with locals. 'I've stayed all over the UK and Orkney is the best place to stay. The people are friendly, there is never any problem. In other places you have to keep hold of your children at all times, but here it's not so important. I would not open a place on the mainland – too much trouble. But you don't get that here.'

Others insisted there was still very much an undercurrent of racism in the community. One former Kirkwall resident later said, 'The murder shocked the entire community. There is no doubt about that but the whole question of racism on the Orkneys is another matter. I believe, as do many others, that Shamsuddin Mahmood died because racism was being encouraged even to young people at a time when it should have been stamped out. That enabled a teenage boy to feel he had the right to shoot dead a man who might have previously irritated him. There is no way that murder would have happened if the target had been white. It's as simple as that. People here need to tackle this issue head on. Not even the racist murder of a man has really put this issue to bed here. You can see it in people's faces when they see a black person walk through main streets of Kirkwall. Many of the locals look on them suspiciously at best and with hatred at worst.'

Allegations that the murder of Mahmood was fuelled by such racial hatred even prompted one of Orkney's top policemen, Chief Inspector David Miller, to concede that there had been other racist attacks on Orkney. He told one journalist, 'We deal with it, if it occurs. It is clear we may, as a community, he accused of being racist. However I strongly believe that we are a community that is strong, diverse and safe. Yes, there is the odd incident that takes place – we are a diverse community.'

Eddy Ross gave an interview and returned to one of his favourite subjects, that of how the Freemasons plotted to ensure Michael was convicted. He claimed the Masons' 'conspiracy' involved serving police officers. Ross said, 'I have been aware that, from the beginning of this case, there has been an undeniable and abhorrent stench emanating from it. That stench was one of collusion, a conspiracy to concoct evidence in order to convict my son of the crime of murder. This collusion was formulated and perpetrated by individuals within the Northern Constabulary and certain persons within the Kirkwall Masonic lodge. We could only have reached the present situation by that collusion being condoned and supported by senior officers of the Northern Constabulary. The collusion is complete and successful. My son has been convicted and awaits a sentence of life imprisonment. The end justified the means.' Detective Constable Bob Petrie, who'd been involved in the murder investigation and was the grand master of the Kirkwall Kilwinning Masonic lodge, refused to comment on Ross's allegations. Meanwhile, supporters of the family set up pages on the Bebo and Facebook social-networking websites, claiming the verdict was wrong and should be overturned.

A week after the verdict, a manager at Glasgow's main Avis car rental office alerted police when he noticed a Ford Fiesta had not been returned and discovered Ross was in jail. Avis found the car through a tracking device in the Tesco car park. But when Avis company staff arrived to take it away, they found the grenade in the glove compartment and called the police, who then stumbled on the arms cache in the boot.

On 11 July, Michael Ross was back in court in Glasgow to be sentenced. He remained stony-faced in the dock as he was told by Judge Lord Hardie he must spend a minimum of twenty-five years behind bars before being eligible for parole. Lord Hardie told him, 'This was a vicious, evil, unprovoked murder of a defenceless man. The attack was a premeditated assassination. The evidence disclosed that you held racist views and sympathy for Nazi Germany. These views were not only abhorrent but an insult to the memory of those including members of your own distinguished regiment, who sacrificed their lives in opposition to them and in support of democratic principles.' Lord Hardie described Mr Mahmood's murder as a 'great loss to his family and friends and the people he served.'

Michael Ross was jailed for a further five years after admitting that he'd attempted to defeat the ends of justice by trying to escape, as well as committing firearms offences. He refused to explain exactly why he'd decided to try and escape. Michael Ross found himself once again about to follow in his father's footsteps.

# 30.

MICHAEL ROSS WASN'T exactly a 'natural fit' in prison, although he managed to get along with inmates he considered important to his safety.

Some saw him as a hero of the right; a man who stood up for his race and had no choice but to take the law into his own hands. But others saw Ross as a deranged, obsessed killer whose complete lack of self-control and empathy led him to think he could get away with killing an innocent man in cold blood just because he didn't like the colour of his skin.

Just like his father before him, prison wasn't such a great hardship for Ross, overall. In the army, he'd been trained on how to deal with incarceration if he was ever kidnapped by terrorists. And Ross no doubt regarded prison as an 'enemy encampment'. He'd clearly promised himself he'd never stop trying to prove his alleged innocence. This steely determination not to show his true feelings may well have marked Michael Ross out as a 'bit dangerous' in the eyes of most other inmates.

THE SNIPER'S STORY

As a result, Ross somehow avoided the day-to-day business of prison life, which usually meant 'doing favours' for other inmates in exchange for certain privileges. This was prison 'currency'. Ross rose above it all and no one had the courage to challenge him, either. The use of drugs in prison appalled him. He shunned any involvement with anything illegal inside. His father had drummed it into him that in order to survive in prison and stand any chance of winning his planned appeal, he had to stay as clean as a whistle. At meal times, other former inmates later revealed, Ross often sat alone in the far corner of the prison canteen. But isolation did not bother him one bit.

When concerned staff and inmates tried to make friends, Ross treated them with deep suspicion. Another spin-off from his intense army training would have been the belief that many inmates were only trying to befriend him in order to advance their own cause inside prison. There are no records of him being involved in any violent altercations with other inmates. No doubt he believed his survival in jail depended on not rising to the bait. Eddy had told him that the prison authorities would like nothing better than to throw him into the isolation wing for the next ten years, as they had tried to do to his father. So, with few inmates prepared to take on the muscly, thirty-year-old squaddie, Ross quickly earned himself a reputation as a hard man. After all, he'd been convicted of murdering an innocent man in cold blood and everyone inside knew that Michael had also totted up numerous kills as a sniper in Iraq.

'Most of us kept well away from him,' one former inmate later recalled.

In November, a few months after Ross's sentencing, police

investigated claims from a woman that she was with him on the night Shamsudden Mahmood was killed. The twenty-seven-year-old told police she and Ross were friends and that they'd been talking on a street in Kirkwall at the time of the shooting. 'If how I remember it is right, then there is no way Michael could have done it,' she said, 'because he was in the gardens speaking to us at the time. I have always remembered it that way. I have never remembered it any differently and it has stayed in my head for that reason, because it's a memorable night.' The woman insisted that the hundred-thousand-pound reward offered for new information by one of Eddy Grant's neighbours in St Ola was not her motive for coming forward. She told reporters, 'I have known the Rosses for a big part of my life. I wouldn't profit out of what they've gone through.' The police did not take her claims seriously.

Back in prison, Ross continued to keep his head down while his father and family supporters began preparing an appeal against the guilty verdict. They intended dissecting every aspect of the case in the hope of finding weak areas that could be used to try and prove Michael's innocence. One family friend later said, 'Michael was warned it could take years to finalise the appeal, so he had to keep calm and not get into any trouble in prison as it would not help his case if he showed he was in any way a defiant inmate.'

Michael Ross obeyed his father's orders, as usual, at least on the surface. Although he was still scheming, again as usual, on all levels, constantly thinking of ways to get his freedom back and put two fingers up at the system.

\* \* \*

During the early years of Michael Ross's incarceration, his supporters, who called themselves J4MR ('Justice for Michael Ross'), gained access to official documents and other material that they saw as highly relevant to the case. They insisted to reporters that this new paperwork significantly strengthened their case for an appeal to clear Ross. The main argument from the Ross camp was that there was no more significant evidence against him than there had been when police first questioned him in the months following the murder. They once again pointed out that the prosecutor had decided back in 1995 there wasn't enough evidence to charge him with the murder. Yet with no significant new information the police continued to pursue the case.

But others in Kirkwall were not so convinced. One said, 'The Ross family and their supporters had nothing to lose but their continued defence of Michael seemed blind to the facts of the case. Many of them thought that if they kept banging away in the end a judge would turn round and pronounce Michael innocent of all charges and he could then go back to the Black Watch regiment and continue his life exactly as it was before he was arrested. It sounded like a pipe-dream.'

Eddy and his family's round-the-clock obsession with proving his son innocent had to be put to one side when his wife Moira was asked to a tea party with the Queen in recognition of her services to cancer care in the community. Moira took Eddy to the Holyrood House reception in Edinburgh. Scottish tabloid newspapers were outraged that 'ex-con' Ross had been 'hobnobbing' with royalty despite his son being in prison for murder. Ross himself was appalled by the negative publicity and even more upset because he didn't want to do anything that might embarrass the Queen. Many in the J4MR group interpreted the Queen's invitation to Moira as yet more evidence that Michael Ross was innocent of murder.

In April 2012, Michael Ross's first appeal was rejected by the appeal court in Edinburgh, although judges described prime witness Willy Grant as a 'less than satisfactory witness'. Ross was devastated by the rejection of his innocence and it seems to have sent him spiraling into depression. He later admitted to feeling like a caged animal, having got into the habit of constantly pacing up and down in his cell. For the first time, Michael Ross must have felt completely hopeless about being ever released. Back in St Ola, Eddy was equally devastated by the rejection. He must have known Michael was on a knife-edge and no doubt feared the effect this would all have on his son's mental health.

Fellow inmates later said that Michael changed, becoming more distant and less communicative with his fellow inmates and prison staff. He was back in planning mode. He was determined to insure there would be some light at the end of the tunnel one day. Around this time, in the middle of 2012, prison authorities became so concerned that Ross might try to break out of prison that he was transferred to a newly opened, maximum-security jail, HMP Shotts. This facility had been specifically constructed for long-term prisoners who were considered security risks. Privately, police and prison officers were no doubt deeply concerned about Ross's state of mind. It was clear that the rejection of his appeal was having a very serious impact on his personality. His entire mindset now seemed to revolve around constantly thinking of ways to escape prison. Some presumed that Ross had given up on ever being ever legitimately freed from prison, so he'd decided to make it his fulltime job to attempt to escape.

Prison psychiatrists who tried to access Michael's emotional state at this time no doubt struggled to get anywhere with him. One of them later described Michael as 'a closed book.' Eddy, Moira and their other children visited Michael at Shotts whenever they could but they couldn't do it on a regular basis because the prison, located between Edinburgh and Glasgow, was not much easier to get to from Orkneys in the north as from London in the south.

Many of those inside HMP Shotts had been behind bars for so long they called the Scottish prison service 'Mum and Dad'. There were more murderers behind Shotts's four walls than in the whole of the rest of Scotland. Twenty-four-hour CCTV monitors ensured that most of the five hundred prisoners remained well-behaved, including a select band of prisoners who would never be released. Ross no doubt felt as hopeless as them. Somehow he had to pull himself up by the boot strings and start making 'plans' for his future.

In the middle of 2013, Eddy Ross broke a self-imposed rule of not speaking to the media and agreed to be interviewed on air by BBC Radio Orkney reporter Dave Gray. Those who heard it later said that thought Ross sounded nervous, almost breathless for much of the interview, which lasted longer than half an hour. Dave Gray later recalled, 'Eddy was very convincing. He was very engaging and charming and not the cold manipulator that others claim he is. There was no feedback from him after the interview. He did not insist on editing it or controlling it in any way. In fact, he was very fair about it all and said to me, "You can ask me anything at all."'

Ross admitted having 9mm weapons and even talked about

the steel container he used to store all his bullets. But he continued to insist that he never at any time thought Michael had been involved in the murder and insisted that many witnesses said that the shooter had been an adult, 'so how could it have been Michael?' However, Ross did insist that Michael had still been fifteen when he was first interviewed by the police. This was not true but it wasn't picked up by the interviewer. Michael had already turned sixteen by the time he was first hauled into Kirkwall police station. Eddy also told the radio station he was still angry that he'd been 'lured' to the police station in December 1994 by officers claiming there had been 'a development' in the case while officers raided his home.

'That's when the police swooped on my house,' an indignant Ross told the radio reporter. 'It was disturbing to say the least.'

He told Dave Gray that he'd warned both his sons to stay out of trouble as teenagers because an arrest might prevent them joining the armed services. Ross continually denied on the programme that a second box of the relevant bullets even existed and in one outburst he said he knew both the police officers who interviewed his son: 'I couldn't understand how they failed to get a confession out of him unless he really didn't do it.' Ross's voice lowered as he talked about the future for himself and his family. 'We've had to go on with our lives. There is not a day goes by when I don't think about what's happened. I could be walking through the town centre or watching TV and suddenly, bang, it's back in my head. It will be with us for ever. But my belief in myself and Michael drives me on.'

# 31.

BY THE EARLY summer of 2014, Michael Ross had spent six years in prison. His supporters, including his father, convinced him to launch a new appeal against his conviction, no doubt in the hope it might lift his spirits. Ross must have known his only chance of winning it was to continue to deny all involvement in the murder.

He'd had plenty of time to think long and hard about his trial and had become convinced that he should have given evidence himself from the dock – if the jury had heard his version of events then they might have felt differently about him. So Ross, usually shy about speaking in public, decided it was time to speak out in advance of this new appeal in the hope it might influence the judges in their decision.

In an open letter to his supporters he declared, 'I did not kill Shamsuddin Mahmood and had nothing to do with his murder.' The letter ran to a thousand words and Ross wrote, 'Before finding out that Shamsuddin had been murdered, I had no knowledge of him and had never encountered him. I sympathise with his family. It would be terrible to lose a loved one in this way and I feel for Shamsuddin and his family as they have still not had justice.'

Ross also said in the letter he was greatly missing his wife and two daughters, now aged eleven and nine. He also lamented the rare opportunities when he was able to see his parents. The letter was later obtained by the Scottish *Sunday Express*, who printed it in full, including Ross's discussion of his sympathy for Mahmood's family and his insistence that claims he was a racist were 'ridiculous and offensive'.

Back in Kirkwall, Ross family supporters latched onto the letter as further proof of his innocence. But others in the community were deeply upset when Ross supporters said that, as part of Michael Ross's appeal, they would be revealing that Shamsuddin Mahmood had at one stage studied Islamic history and this made him a more 'sinister' character – as if that somehow warranted his murder. Ross supporters also claimed that Mahmood had been lying about his university education and was very poorly educated compared to the rest of his family and this was a matter of great shame for him. They also insisted that the police had used 'unfair tactics' when interviewing Ross and claimed detectives had run an oppressive campaign against him in order to prosecute him for murder.

At the British Legion in Kirkwall, long-standing member Eddy Ross was elevated to club chairman, which gave him even more status in the community despite the fact his oldest son had been convicted of murder. As one member later said, 'Being made chairman was quite an achievement for Eddy. Many members still believed Michael was innocent and this was their way of showing their appreciation and understanding of Eddy Ross and why he believed there had been a huge miscarriage of justice. It also gave Eddy a boost. He could hold his head up even higher and point to the Legion as showing him their full support and loyalty.'

Loyalty was very important to Eddy Ross.

At HMP Shotts, Michael Ross initially grew more hopeful that his new appeal might be successful. However, there were still some days when he must have felt doomed to spend much of the rest of his life in prison. His family and friends no doubt believed in this new appeal. Also, it would help him cope with life in prison if he felt there was still a chance he would be found innocent. But then he was informed that this latest appeal would take three years to come to fruition, as supporters tried to gather in more new evidence. T They claimed the police were wrong to use a dramatic reconstruction clip of Michael Ross in Papdale Woods for the *Crimewatch UK* broadcast following the murder because it might have prejudiced his trial. The long wait for the appeal seemed to have sent Michael Ross nose-diving into a new emotional meltdown.

Other inmates and staff began noticing how edgy he had become and eventually he was examined by a doctor, who decided that he needed hospital treatment.

On 6 August 2014, Michael Ross was taken by prison van from Shotts prison and driven to the local hospital, Monklands, in North Lanarkshire. When the van stopped at traffic lights, Michael Ross rose from his 'sickbed' and attacked his guards. Somehow, they managed to overpower him as the ambulance stopped in a lay-by. Police were immediately called to the scene and launched an investigation. Michael

Ross returned to HMP Shotts as an even bigger security risk. Many of his privileges were taken away and he became even more distant from other inmates.

In November the following year, Ross's appeal was quashed. The three-year investigation by the Scottish Criminal Cases Review Commission found that the police investigation hadn't been oppressive and that Michael Ross's police interviews had been fairly conducted. The Scottish Criminal Cases Review Commission (SCCRC) also said the police had been completely justified in using that dramatic reconstruction clip of Michael Ross in Papdale Woods for the TV broadcast because Michael had not at that stage been confirmed as having been the person in Papdale Woods. No doubt Ross's sense of isolation and hopelessness increased after the appeal rejection.

In September 2016, he stole a saw from the prison workshop, having swapped it for a wooden replica that he had spent weeks constructing. The replica was spotted by two prison guards doing an audit in the workshop. No one knows how Michael Ross intended to use the saw but when other inmates were confronted by the guards about who had made the replica, he immediately stepped forward and admitted it was him.

His life-long obsession with always having a plan had most likely led him to kill a man in cold blood. Now Ross was using that same mindset to constantly plan ways to try and escape from prison. What did he have to lose? Many believe that he genuinely believed it was his 'duty' to try and escape in the same way that prisoners-of-war attempt to flee their captors. As long as Ross could tell himself he was a wrongly imprisoned soldier then maybe he could hope one day to be freed.

A few weeks after his latest escape attempt, Ross refused to allow TV cameras into his cell as part of a TV documentary about HMP Shotts that was to feature men who'd committed some of Scotland most heinous crimes. Ross was outraged to be classified as one of 'them'. He and his father considered themselves to be victims of a police framing and they were going to continue to protest their innocence to anyone prepared to listen. Appearing on a TV programme about convicted criminals was not going to help Michael Ross's cause one bit.

In January 2018, inmates at Shotts rioted and attacked prison guards with pool cues after a row about whether they could watch live darts or football on TV. Ross studiously avoided any involvement in the disturbances. He also wasn't much of a sports fan.

By March of that year, J4MR announced it had raised over twenty thousand pounds from an online crowdfunding appeal to pay for specialist solicitors to continue to try and prove Ross was innocent. Campaigners insisted that he should be cleared because witnesses described the killer as being around six foot tall and Ross was five feet and seven inches. This was not strictly speaking accurate but the group seemed to have locked onto the doubt that some witnesses had about the killer's height.

The J4MR group even continued to show understanding for Ross's reasons for trying to escape. One supporter told reporters, 'He has, at times, acted out of desperation and perhaps not helped his case for innocence in the eyes of many. Despite this, we must remember that he was a child of fifteen at the time of the original crime and there is not one single aspect of the weak circumstantial case against him that cannot be discredited.'

The ultimate aim of the J4MR group was for human rights lawyers to gather enough evidence to submit an updated case to SCCRC with a view to gaining a referral to the Court of Appeal. They also planned to submit a detailed complaint to the Police Investigations and Review Commission (PIRC) in Scotland.

But many in the Orkneys wished the supporters of the Ross family would now give up their 'hopeless' fight for justice and enable the islands to regain their self-respect.

# 32.

BY JUNE 2018, Eddy Ross and the J4MR group were growing increasingly concerned that the case was no longer attracting enough attention. Ross informed reporters he was impressed by his son's new laidback attitude inside prison, as if that somehow implied Michael was innocent.

Eddy also claimed to the family's supporters for the first time that a senior police officer had assured him many years earlier that there was no concrete evidence against his son. Many wondered why he had taken so long to reveal this.

Glasgow-based human rights lawyer Aamer Anwar agreed to take on Michael Ross's case after he met with him in Shotts prison. Ross must have been delighted to have something new to cling on to in relation to his innocence. In a statement from prison through the J4MR group, Ross said, '[Aamer's] been very realistic with me and I know it won't be an easy task to get my case to the next stage. I have to trust someone to take my case forward. I believe that he understands the issues with my conviction. It's hard for me to have any faith in the system, but I do think he'll try hard for me.'

A spokeswoman for the J4MR group issued their own statement: 'We just want Michael out of prison and home to his family where he can start rebuilding his life. If anyone can help him, we believe it's Aamer Anwar.'

But a few weeks later 'laidback' Michael Ross surprised inmates and staff at HMP Shotts by attempting a third escape. This time he tried to scale a fence. People were starting to ask if Ross was simply making a plea for help. Maybe it was time to stop all the appeals and allow him to serve his sentence with dignity. But Eddy Ross and the family's supporters wouldn't even entertain such a notion.

On 8 August, Ross spoke publicly about his three failed escape attempts. In an interview with a Scottish daily newspaper, he said, 'For me, planning an escape is like seeing an open door to the outside world. For me not to take that opportunity to walk through the door is madness. It's only natural for captive animals to want to get out of their enclosure.' He also insisted those attempts to flee proved his innocence rather than his guilt. Others were saying that Ross had for the first time since the murder begun to lose faith in his own ability to achieve what he considered to be justice. Ross himself said, 'Now having served ten years in jail I'm back at the beginning again, but much worse as I have to rely on my lawyers finding a new approach that will be acceptable within the narrow constraints of criminal appeals processes. The hardest thing for me in my recent actions is the thought of the upset I may have caused my family, friends and my supporters.'

After his third attempt, Ross had been hauled before a group of independent prison governors. Instead of bowing down to them he informed them, 'You should be doing more to allow prisoners opportunities to bring focus onto their cases if it's a potential miscarriage of justice.'

A few weeks later Michael Ross turned forty and, presumably as part of his new strategy under Aamer Anwar, he continued issuing regular statements from his prison cell. He still considered himself a freedom fighter, so his attempted prison escapes were just another way of highlighting his search for justice. Speaking through his campaign group, he said, 'I don't do these things without thought or with a careless attitude, although it may seem like that. I think that the general public opinion is that all prisoners are guilty, but all claim to be innocent.' Ross conceded once again that his escape attempts had damaged his fight for innocence. 'I don't mean any disrespect to all those that are working hard on my campaign, and I do feel like all of these brilliant efforts will make for success eventually. The hardest thing for me in my recent actions is the thought of the upset I may have caused my family, friends and my supporters.'

Ross's interviews seemed to imply that he still remained the professional soldier who saw escaping as 'taking action' in the belief that it made him look different from normal prisoners. Michael Ross was a man of action, someone who believed – just like his father Eddy – that he could beat the system.

Meanwhile, campaigners for J4MR announced they still aimed to submit an updated case to the SCCRC with a view to gaining a referral to the Court of Appeal once again and clearing Michael Ross's name.

A spokeswoman for J4MR said, 'Michael has now spent

a quarter of his life locked up in prison for a crime he says he did not commit. The evidence against him was weak and circumstantial and can all be discredited. We know that some people that were involved with the original police investigation and the subsequent cold-case review have information that could turn this case around and potentially lead to the murder conviction being quashed.'

It seemed to many that Michael Ross really was like a caged animal: one side of him wanted desperately to continue to claim his innocence, while another side simply wanted to head for the hills, armed to the teeth with deadly weapons and disappear for the rest of his life.

# Epilogue

THE TWENTY-FIFTH anniversary of the murder of Shamsuddin Mahmood was on 2 June 2019.

While sifting through police reports, listening to witness accounts and finally knitting this extraordinary story together, I became completely immersed in the subject. I've thought through so many elements and claims in terms of the victim and the alleged perpetrator. And it has left me with a real sense of knowing how this crime came to be committed.

The failure to properly consider the victim and his family is undeniable. The failure to find his killer for so long left lasting disquiet. But in breezy St Ola – high above Kirkwall – remain Michael Ross's father Eddy and mother Moira. They invited me in to their home to talk about the case on a typically blustery day in early January 2019. Both were reluctant to help but in the end furnished me with some of the most personal of details that have been used in the book.

However, at the end of the day this story revolves around

the extraordinary way in which a bond between a caring father and his son seems to have gone off course with deadly consequences. As one behavioral psychiatrist said, 'It's possible that Michael simply lost the ability to tell the difference between right and wrong because of his need to please his father during his childhood.' The saddest aspect of this entire story is that Eddy Ross no doubt saw himself as a good father trying to ensure his son succeeded in later life. But in the end did the lines between good and bad become so blurred that they both ended up being partners in crime?

During the month of my visit, the Orkneys grabbed the media spotlight for all the right reasons when it was named the best place to live in the UK in an annual survey. The Halifax bank's quality-of-life survey ranked the islands above all other areas of the UK, with Richmondshire in Yorkshire in second place, followed by Rutland in the Midlands, Hambleton in Yorkshire and Eden in Cumbria in fifth place. The Orkneys' elevation was based on its high employment levels, low crime rate, strong exam results, smaller primary class sizes and good health and happiness scores. Many local people are today proud that Orkney seems to have finally recovered its self-esteem following the murder of Shamsuddin Mahmood, which had tainted the islands for almost a quarter of a century.

But, unfortunately, the appalling spectre of racism still exists on the islands as it does throughout the world. And the ghosts of those brave servicemen who drowned at the hands of *U-47* seem destined to haunt this strange, isolated land for ever.

*If Michael was here at the moment, he'd be like me.*
*Very disciplined but a wee bonnier than me.*

Eddy Ross